The River Cottage

Fruit Handbook

The River Cottage Fruit Handbook

by Mark Diacono

with an introduction by

Hugh Fearnley-Whittingstall

www.rivercottage.net

BLOOMSBURY

LONDON · BERLIN · NEW YORK · SYDNEY

For my mum

First published in Great Britain 2011

Text and photography copyright © 2011 by Mark Diacono
Illustrations © 2011 by Toby Atkins

The moral right of the author has been asserted

Bloomsbury Publishing Plc, 36 Soho Square, London W1D 3QY
Bloomsbury Publishing, London, Berlin, New York and Sydney

A CIP catalogue record for this book is available from the British Library

ISBN 978 1 4088 0881 8
10 9 8 7 6 5 4 3 2 1

Project Editor: Janet Illsley
Designer: Will Webb
Illustrator: Toby Atkins

Printed and bound in Italy by Graphicom

MIX
Paper from
responsible sources
FSC® C013123

www.bloomsbury.com/rivercottage

Contents

It's no secret that I'm an absolute fruit fiend. I revel in the stuff, I am in awe of its utter deliciousness and its evolutionary neatness. If one food was designed, unambiguously, to be eaten, then surely it has to be fruit. We consume it, we spread the seed, more fruit grows, everyone's happy. It's in Nature's best interests to make it as enticing as possible and she's certainly done so. Fruit is a real treat that often needs no embellishment and is resoundingly, unequivocally good for us. Mark Diacono's first River Cottage handbook, *Veg Patch*, was a joy: a thorough, yet accessible guide to raising homegrown produce that has established Mark as one of the foremost thinkers and writers on the subject of growing what you eat. Now he's turned his attention to fruit and, as you're about to discover, has written another confidence-inspiring, anxiety-reducing little gem... or perhaps that should be little peach.

It's no mean feat, because getting people to grow their own fruit presents particular challenges. In many ways it's the last frontier of domestic horticulture. While there's been a revolution in the growing of vegetables and herbs in the UK in recent years, home fruit growing has lagged a little behind. I suspect this is because there's a certain air of mystery attached to growing fruit, a sense that specialist knowledge and hard-won skills must be acquired before one can make a go of it. Also, being that much more delicate and squashable than a celeriac or a carrot, a raspberry or a plum can appear to need rather more cosseting. In his gardening courses at River Cottage, I've seen Mark banish these myths and give people the confidence to start producing their own berries, apples, plums, melons and apricots. This book, I know, will do the same thing. As Mark explains, fruit wants to grow – you just have to let it – and he's here to show you how.

It's a common mantra – and how could I not endorse it – that we should all be eating fruit every day, ideally several times a day. It is one of the easiest ways to add goodness, sweetness, colour and flavour to our diets. More than any other food, it makes us feel good in body and soul. Yet so often our fruit hails from far afield, cling-wrapped and air-freighted from some tropical clime, or super-chilled in little plastic punnets and transported from the far end of the country. I'm not about to advocate that we all give up bananas and oranges, but there are so many fruits that can grow successfully in our own backyards, and I think we should give them precedence. Buying seasonal British fruit from a local farm shop, a pick-your-own farm or a good greengrocer is a very sound choice. But there is no more sustainable, and no more pleasing way to put fruit on the table than to grow it yourself.

I believe that everyone should have some fruit growing within their reach, for at least part of the year. You don't even need a garden to achieve this: a couple of blueberry bushes in a big pot on a patio, or a window box of alpine strawberries, is easy to maintain and delightful to plunder. If you have even a small garden, you can do much more: tiny plots can foster small, but very productive fruit trees, as well as compact currant bushes. Your location needn't hold you back either. In fact, as Mark points out, the urban or suburban gardener often has an advantage over the rural dweller when it comes to fruit growing. A sun-trap patio or roof garden can provide a microclimate where nectarines, apricots or greengages will flourish much more readily than they would in a windswept country acre. If you have anything approaching a regular-sized veg patch you can easily produce more fruit than you can immediately eat: a moderate garden can comfortably support a plum, a pear and an apple tree, plus several soft fruit bushes. Providing you get the hang of storing apples (not difficult, as Mark explains), and if you have a freezer, this can give you fruit from the end of May until well after Christmas.

In the first instance, I hope you will greedily peruse this book as one would a menu. Feast your eyes on the many different varieties of fruit that can be grown in this country and then think about the ones that appeal most to you. Mark's perennial advice, which I heartily second, is that you should only grow what you like to eat. But with that in mind, you may want to ask yourself: are you sure you know what you like to eat? Or, to put it another way, keep an open mind, and an open mouth! It's easy to dismiss a lot of fruit – even strawberries, plums and pears – if you've only ever tried one bland, under-ripe supermarket variety. But a sun-warmed 'Royal Sovereign' strawberry or a perfectly ripe 'Doyenne du Comice' pear could completely change your mind.

And if you think you don't like apples, I'd have to suggest that you simply haven't met the right apple for you yet. There are hundreds of varieties to choose from. I'm a bit of an apple fascist myself, favouring the crisp and the sharp – nothing soft, woolly or too sweet for me – so I grow the delectable 'Ashmead's Kernel' in my garden, as well as 'Orleans Reinette', 'Blenheim Orange' and 'Lord Lambourne'. I'm lucky to have the space to do that, but it's possible now, through the wonders of modern grafting techniques, to have an apple tree which produces up to four different varieties of apple. You could produce Cox's, Bramleys, Russets and, dare I say, 'Ashmead's Kernel', all on one bit of tailormade rootstock.

I reckon there's a latent fruit grower lurking in all of us, even if we don't know it yet. This book, shot through as it is with Mark's customary 'just do it' attitude, will surely release it. Never one to let the grass grow under his feet, or to beat around the (gooseberry) bush, Mark demonstrates that fruit growing is neither an arcane science or a hopeless fantasy, but an entirely do-able and unbelievably satisfying undertaking that will enrich your life, and your diet, in untold ways. So never mind the skin and pips – they're all part of the pleasure – just take a big bite of luscious, fruity flesh, and let the juice trickle down your chin.

Hugh Fearnley-Whittingstall, East Devon, May 2011

Growing your
own Fruit

The taste of homegrown juicy peaches, aromatic plums, crisp bright early apples and the sweet-sharp of the summer's strawberries are, I promise you, some of life's richest pleasures. The depth of flavour, scent and succulence that comes with your own fruit, enjoyed in the garden that grew it, is so far from the fruit you can buy that, once tasted, you'll be reluctant to go back.

You'll find yourself trying to squeeze in a currant here, a berry there or a fan-trained tree against a wall. Even a few pots of fruit can open a whole world of flavour that's exclusive to the home grower. Mulberries, Japanese wineberries, damsons and medlars are rarely, if ever, in the shops. Even apples, the commonest of the tree fruit, can be a revelation grown at home as you can take your pick from thousands of varieties to suit your taste buds and your location.

And if you get it right you can enjoy something different every month: forced rhubarb from March, stone fruit, berries and currants in the summertime, through to autumn with the late ripeners – grapes and figs among them – and into winter with quince, medlars and the stored-to-ripen apples and pears.

Add to that the pleasures of preserving some of those flavours in jams, chutneys, leathers, syrups, vodkas and vinegars and you'll be enjoying your own fruit for months, if not years ahead.

Flavour isn't the only reward. You may find that the fruit you pick isn't so much the whole point of growing it as one of a chain of pleasures that comes along the way. The medlar's lazy flowers, the house-filling perfume of ripening quince and the shock of cherry blossom across a tree in spring lift the soul as much as any ornamental plant.

Starting up can be more costly with fruit than it is for vegetables. There are trees and bushes that you may wish to buy, some tools too, but most fruit plants deliver for years and investment now will save you a fortune over time. After the initial outlay you'll be in for virtually free harvests year after year. Fruit is generally expensive to buy and growing your own insulates you against rising prices, while giving you the finest fruit there is.

Fruit is a longer game than veg, so take time to consider what you're planting. You can always drop vegetables after a summer of fun but with fruit it's marriage. Planting a bush or a tree makes a statement – it says I'm here and I intend to stay... or at the very least, I'm here and I care enough about those who follow to plant this tree. You choose, plant and care for something that could be with you for years, generations even.

It's not one-way traffic though. Grow some fruit and we are, of course, falling for the oldest trick in the book. Like most plants, a fruit plant produces seeds in the hope of succeeding in its one true aim – to replicate itself. If all those seeds fell in the shade of the parent's branches, the competition and lack of light would doom most to failure, so plants have developed strategies for getting the seeds

further afield. Some use the wind, others hitch a ride on the fur of passing animals, while many produce a delicious coating around the seed which entices wild animals and us humans to tuck in. We devour the fruit largely oblivious that it is at its peak of delicious ripeness precisely because the seed is in the ideal state for travel. We sink our teeth in and the discarded or excreted seeds make it beyond the umbrella of the plant. It is the perfect bribe and everybody wins.

Fruit is naturally low carbon. Almost all fruit plants are perennial – they grow and produce year after year rather than being sown afresh every spring as most vegetables are. There's no need to buy fresh seed nor cultivate the soil each year, and once the plant is established it has the engine room below ground and above to get on with growing quickly when the starter's gun fires in spring.

Where a veg patch needs constant input, most fruit gets by with minimal care. As a result, perennials are much more capable than annual plants of growing well without man-made fertilisers. This is an important point. Our reliance on fossil fuels is the major cause of climate change and the way we feed ourselves accounts for almost a third of our carbon footprint. So reliant are we on the man-made fertilisers (made with vast quantities of oil and water) and so extended is the supply chain from plot to plate that for every unit of energy we gain from our food, we use 10 units in growing it and getting it to our table.

Growing fruit also offers a more secure food supply. Ninety per cent of the fruit we eat in the UK is imported. If that doesn't shock you or you think that figure may be comprised mainly of exotic fruit that we are unable to grow for ourselves, bear in mind that three-quarters of our apples – a fruit perfectly suited to growing in our climate – come from overseas, while many of our orchards stand with their fruit unharvested. It's an extraordinary state of affairs and one that leaves us vulnerable to shortages and rising prices elsewhere, especially when most of the chemicals and energy we use to grow fruit in the UK is also imported.

Growing your own fruit may seem insignificant in the face of such global issues, but it is millions of tiny votes cast every day when we shop that has given us such a carbon-heavy food supply. Each time we grow a little it is a vote for a future which has a local, low-carbon diet at its heart. And local doesn't get any more local than homegrown.

'Local' even tastes better. Of the thousands of apple varieties we can feast on, we make do largely with a handful of long-life so-so favourites, such as Fuji, which can last for 6 months with refrigeration. Symmetrical and unblotched, they are visually seductive, they even taste ok, but when there are so many outstanding apples out there, why settle for ok? It's a similar story for pears, plums and many others. Local varieties suit local conditions and they tend to do well without chemical inputs, while adding biodiversity value and character to the landscape. It's a winner on every level.

Of course we can't hope to grow all the fruit we eat, but growing what best suits our soils and climate, while still trading for the lemons, oranges and other exotics that can't be grown (at least sustainably) in this country, has to be part of how we feed ourselves in the future. And you planting some fruit is a real step towards it.

This is a food book, driven by how we use fruit in the kitchen. It wasn't written in Pedants' Corner. You know what makes a fruit a fruit and a vegetable a vegetable – and tomatoes are most definitely not in this book. My aim is to help and encourage you to grow some fruit and to make the experience as trouble-free and delicious as possible. I could have happily written a book for each fruit but what you have in your hands is a guide to what you have to do, some of the important options and as much personal experience as it seems sensible to impart.

I have offered you a few ideas of what to do with each fruit to get the best out of them in the kitchen, plus some recipes which are happily adaptable to many other fruit. Do nose around on the internet, speak to allotmenters, gardeners and nursery owners, and follow a few bloggers who are out there doing it for themselves. Other people's experiences is well worth learning from but don't be afraid to go your own way and experiment if you feel the urge.

We are blessed with living in interesting if challenging times, and for many growing some of what we eat feels like a good thing to do. The wave of interest in doing just that in the last decade isn't just people looking for an antidote to city life, or a burst of nostalgia – these are people who find that growing some of what you eat enriches your life in many (often unexpected) ways. This is not a passing moment but an enduring movement, the early steps in a more sane and delicious way of eating. The next decades will see individuals, families and communities building on what the pioneers are doing now – allotments, edible back gardens, living roofs, forest gardens, Community Supported Agriculture, village orchards and city farms are just the beginning. And fruit is right at the heart of it.

Essential to life as it is, there is something luxurious about fruit, especially when grown for yourself. Fruit is satisfying to grow in a different way from vegetables, as Jane Grigson observed:

'This special feeling towards fruit, its glory and abundance, is I would say universal... we respond to strawberry fields or cherry orchards with a delight that a cabbage patch or even an elegant vegetable garden cannot provoke.'

Fruit plants lace the years together, growing along with you and your loved ones. They bring unexpected pleasures. Much as I love my veg patch, there's a different kind of happiness that comes with seeing the fruit trees I planted when my daughter was waiting to be born that she now plays beneath, picks and eats the fruit from and one day soon will be climbing in.

I hope you'll grow some.

Choosing what to grow

Deciding which fruit to invite into your garden, allotment or collection of pots is a big decision. The plants may be with you for years and take up a reasonable amount of space. Fruit plants are often costly – that's not to say expensive in the long term. When you look at likely harvests over the lifespan of the plant, the plant itself is often little short of a bargain, but there is still a substantial initial outlay. There may be a little wait while the plant gets up to full productivity, so you'll want to be looking forward to its fruit and not disappointed when it arrives. A wish list is vital.

Make a list of whichever fruit takes your fancy. Don't be hamstrung by practical considerations such as space or climate at this point; you may be surprised by what new varieties or dwarfing rootstocks can make possible. Write down your favourites first, discover some others you like the sound of by reading through the Fruit A–Z (pp.28–121), and whittle the list down based on practicalities if you have to.

There are a number of factors I'd suggest you consider when trying to come up with your fruity wish list.

Grow what you most like to eat

This should be a mantra that constantly sings in the back of your mind when planning what to grow. Grow some of your favourite food and you'll look forward to every harvest time, success will be delicious and any expense or effort along the way will feel worth it. Don't feel compelled to grow something you think only OK, simply because it's popular – if apples are 'fine' to you, try something else you love. That said...

Challenge your taste buds

Do look to open the larder door a little, to welcome a few new flavours into your kitchen. With vegetables I always suggest growing two things you dislike (as homegrown veg can be so very different from shop-bought) and two things you've not tasted (better still, never heard of) each year, but with fruit it's not so simple. It is more of a waste to dig up a plum tree when you've confirmed your dislike of them than it is to give your harvest of Brussels sprouts to a neighbour and vow never to grow them again. But the principle of trying new flavours, of seeing whether growing the best varieties for yourself can be so much superior to those you buy in the shops stands.

It's certainly worthwhile trying fruit that's new to you, or that you think you dislike, before you invest in a plant. Visit nurseries and allotments, nose around on the internet and seek advice from local groups and organisations to find the best locally grown fruit to try. Obviously the more money and land you have at your

'Peregrine' peach, fan-trained against a wall

Dittisham plums

disposal the more you can take a risk on an unknown or disliked fruit, but whatever your situation, do stay inquisitive about fruit.

Prioritise the unbuyables

A consideration I always let wander across my brain is whether I can buy a particular fruit locally or in the shops, and if so whether the best varieties are available. It doesn't mean I won't grow it if it's in the shops – a barrowful of homegrown Victoria plums is not hard to enjoy even if you can buy them in town – but there are often others as good that you can grow instead and still enjoy Victorias from the shops. It's how I came across the Dittisham plum, which has given me as much pleasure as any fruit I've grown. As with big maincrop potatoes, there are many apple varieties that are largely indistinguishable from those you can buy and I can see little reason for growing these varieties when there are other incredible cultivars out there screaming for your attention.

Similarly, you may be unfamiliar with quince, medlars or mulberries as they're rarely to be found for sale. This has nothing to do with their flavour; it's partly that they went out of fashion and partly because they don't suit the supermarket supply chain – mulberries, for example, should be picked when perfectly ripe, when they are devilishly delicate and far from robust enough to make the long journey to the supermarket shelves. All three are truly wonderful.

Complement the wild harvest

Even if you live in the city, you are likely to have some forageable fruit nearby – blackberries, apples and plums being among the most likely. If you do, consider whether you really need to grow more in your garden. You may even choose to grow fruit specifically to go with a hedgerow treat – gooseberries to go with foraged elderflowers for one. Please do lay your hands on John Wright's *Hedgerow* handbook to open the door to what may be on your doorstep – together with your garden's crop it'll give you the widest of fruity possibilities.

Grow the expensive fruit

Most fruit is costly, more so when it has a short season and labour-intensive production. Forced rhubarb comes early and sweet and is one of the great fruit treats of the year. Its price reflects a degree of palaver and a brief season of harvest, yet it is simple and cheap to grow this delight for yourself. Blueberries, quince, grapes and figs are also among the more expensive fruit: if you love any of them, then there's a strong claim to a place on your wish list on cost alone.

List the food you love to eat or would like to try and check it against your shopping receipts and online suppliers and consider whether to prioritise the most expensive ahead of some of the cheaper fruit.

Japanese plum in blossom

Consider diversity and succession

Look at your emerging wish list and ask yourself if you have a breadth of flavours. Some bright early apples, a few rich plums, sour gooseberries and some sharp yet sweet raspberries, for example. Or perhaps you'd rather go for a larger harvest of fewer fruit by having either more plants of one type or a spread of varieties of one fruit. Either way is fine, whichever suits you best, but do consciously consider the degree of diversity in your garden.

For each of the fruit on your wish list, use the chart on pp.32–3 to map out when you are likely to be picking your fruit. The only rule is that you are prepared for what's coming – gluts are no better or worse than a steadier supply, but you shouldn't be taken unawares. If the apples all seem to be coming at once and you'd like them more steadily, you may need to alter your choice of varieties.

Grow something beautiful

By 'beautiful' I don't just mean a plant that's pleasing to the eye – I mean create a space that you'd like to spend time in. If it's the place you're drawn to read the paper, have a picnic, a glass of wine or catch an afternoon snooze then you're likely to find it becoming a central part of your life.

It's also worth considering how your plants will look through the year. Most look appetising enough when in fruit, but check the variety descriptions and you may just get fabulous autumnal foliage or stunning flowers as an added bonus. And if you're unsure about whether to go for a Japanese wineberry or a blackberry, it may be the wineberry's furry red/pink winter canes that make the difference.

Consider degrees of risk

Almost all the fruit in this book will grow happily in any part of the UK, but there are a few which are more accustomed to long, hot summers in their natural home. Peaches, nectarines, apricots, figs and grapes are undoubtedly more risky the further north you live but with these less reliable fruit the importance of the microclimate cannot be understated. An apricot trained against a sunny, south-facing wall with shelter from winter and early spring winds grown in Lancashire is likely to have more chance of fruiting well than a freestanding tree exposed to harsh winds in Cornwall.

There are no mathematical formulae for success – just a few elements you have to ensure are favourable if you want to tackle any of the riskier fruit in a more northerly location or at a higher altitude. The rest is a matter for your sense of risk and whether you feel lucky.

One thing that is vital to success, especially in marginal locations, is your choice of variety. The Fruit A–Z (pp.28–121) includes those I think are best for each fruit, but some general principles apply, as follows.

Choosing varieties

Once you have your wish list in place, you'll need to consider which variety of each fruit you are going to plant. This is a critical step as it can guide what time of year you'll be eating your fruit, what that fruit tastes like, the shape of the plant and even the degree of trouble pests may give you. It is the single decision that will most determine how satisfied you will be with your produce. Spend as much time selecting a variety as you have choosing the type of fruit itself. Here are a few pointers to getting the best ones for you.

On the whole, commercial growers prioritise disease resistance, yield and consistency of appearance. All are fine characteristics, but I'd encourage you to put flavour above all. If you can get the other three to fall handily into line behind outstanding flavour then you have the ideal, but if you ask me, a smaller crop of delicious fruit trumps a skipful from a plain variety every time. Do read descriptions, seek advice from suppliers and, most importantly, talk to other growers before you go over your pencilled list in pen.

Many varieties of fruit require another nearby for pollination. Plenty of others do not. If you have room for only one tree, choose a self-fertile variety (i.e. a tree that can pollinate itself) if these are available. Otherwise you'll need to ensure that flowering at least partially overlaps. To help you with this, if you are planning to grow apples, varieties are organised into pollination groups and most good suppliers will indicate this in their catalogue, on their website and on their plant label. Whether this is done with letters (A–H) or numbers (1–8), the key is to choose varieties that coincide or are adjacent (for example, Pollination Group 3 will pollinate trees from Groups 2, 3 and 4). Even self-fertile varieties will usually give you a better harvest if cross-pollinated.

Consider varieties that ripen successionally. Planting three apple trees – one an early-, one a mid- and one a late-season apple – will keep you in fruit over a long, long period and help avoid huge gluts. Of course, if you want to eat or process bigger harvests, the opposite is true. Either way, take a few minutes to marry up how you want your food to be ready with your choice of varieties. The Fruit A–Z (pp.28–121) offers guidance for each of the fruits where relevant, and a good supplier will also be able to advise.

This brings me to my final piece of advice: make friends with good nurseries. There are some excellent nurseries, many of which are in the Directory (see p.248), but check locally too. The best nurseries will give you advice about the ideal rootstocks, varieties and combinations for your location and conditions. They care that you come back, that their plants give you pleasure and perform as they should. They should happily send you elsewhere if there is a plant that somebody else sells that suits you better than their own stock.

Redcurrant grown as a standard

Essential tools

There are many tools out there; some you will call on most weeks if not most days, others are very particular to specific tasks. The list below includes those you are most likely to consider.

When it comes to tools you have a choice: buy well once and enjoy your investment every time you use it, or go cheap and cheerless and regret the inadequacies every time it's in your hand.

If you are on a budget and not growing many plants you may decide to spend a little less on your tools. If so, then make every effort to do as you would with top-quality tools: keep blades sharp, joints oiled and everything clean – to get some proper service from them. Not only will they do a better job, making cleaner cuts that are less likely to invite disease, but the experience of using good tools adds to the pleasure rather than contributing to a chore.

There are, of course, various other garden tools you may find yourself calling on, depending what you choose to grow. A shredder, a hoe, a rake, a water butt, a rubber-ended mallet for knocking in stakes, tree ties, as well as tree guards against rabbits and deer spring to mind.

And don't forget a sharpening stone for keeping blades keen.

Secateurs A sort of heavy-duty pair of mini garden shears, secateurs are a vital tool as they are used for more plant cutting tasks than any other implement. They easily cut through branches up to 1cm across. I'm not supposed to have favourites but Felco's (see Directory, p.249) are the best by an absolute mile.

Loppers Effectively heavy-duty secateurs on long (often extendable) handles that give you extra reach and leverage when pruning in hard-to-access places. Some loppers come with a racheting action that allows you to prune your way through thicker branches more easily.

Penknife There are any number of garden-related knives available – designed specifically for grafting, pruning and other individual tasks. Buy the specialist ones if you find you are doing those tasks regularly; otherwise keep a well-made penknife – always sharp – in your pocket every time you go into your garden. As well as coming in handy for tidying up minor damage or untidy cuts, a knife can be quickly employed whenever you see a need for it, including minor pruning, taking cuttings and cutting string.

Pruning saw A pruning saw is required for cutting through branches of a larger diameter. These curved mini-saws are usually tapered to allow you to prune in tighter areas, and may have single or double-edged blades. Either is fine. You may use a pruning saw less frequently than secateurs but it is likely to be operating under considerable force when you do, so get the best you can afford – you'll be glad you did. Unless you have mature plants that need sawing already, you will be able to delay buying a saw for a few years until your trees have matured a little, so the expense needn't be at the beginning.

Fork The workhorse that takes the brunt of any soil turning or plant lifting. Excellent for turning compost and incorporating compost or manure into the soil. A good-quality fork is a sound investment.

Spade Used for digging, cutting straight edges and turning compost that is too fine to fork.

Trowel and hand fork An elementary set of tools for small-scale, in-close digging, soil turning and weeding.

Wheelbarrow, watering can and two buckets or trugs You'll use all of these for any number of tasks, especially at planting time.

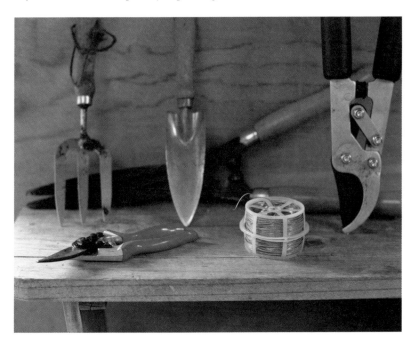

Essential terms

As with many things, growing fruit comes with its share of jargon. It helps to be familiar with the terms that crop up fairly often.

Annual A plant that lives for one year only.

Anther The male part of a flower, which bears pollen.

Bare root A plant sold without soil (or with very little) around its roots.

Biennial bearing Where a plant produces fruit every 2 years.

Biological control A means of controlling pest numbers using their predators and/or parasites.

Bush trees Trees that have a short trunk, 90cm at most, from which branches spread to form a low canopy.

Cordon A tree or bush trained as a single stem (occasionally two or three,) against a wall and/or wire support.

Cultivar Shortened from 'cultivated variety', a term initially used to indicate a variety that had originated in cultivation rather than one found in the wild, but now used (as it is in this book) interchangeably with 'variety'.

Dwarf A fruit tree or bush kept to a smaller size, either by restricting its root space or by grafting it on the rootstock of a smaller species. Dwarf trees enable fruit to be grown in restricted spaces – in tubs on patios, for example.

Ericaceous compost Compost with a pH below 7, ideally suited to plants that thrive in acidic conditions (such as blueberries).

Espalier A tree or bush trained with a single vertical trunk and horizontal laterals – almost always using wire support, often against a wall.

Family tree A tree with more than one variety grafted onto the rootstock, which – if compatible varieties are chosen – can ensure that a single tree takes care of its own pollination, and gives harvests of more than one variety.

Fan A tree or bush trained with branches radiating from a short trunk.

Dwarf peach 'Bonanza' in blossom

Foliar feeding Applying a nourishing solution to a plant's leaves. High potassium feeds (such as seaweed feed and comfrey tea) are very effective when sprayed on the leaves of many fruiting plants from flowering onwards.

Forcing Accelerating a plant's growth, usually by excluding light and/or using heat. Rhubarb (see p.115) and chicory are the most commonly forced edible plants.

Graft The union (usually slightly swollen) on a plant where the scion and the rootstock have been joined. Also describes the act of joining a rootstock to a scion.

Half-standards Trees (and occasionally currant and gooseberry bushes) with a clear trunk (i.e. no branches) of around 1.5m.

June drop Some fruit plants (apple, pear and plum, for example) may shed some of their immature fruit in early summer. Whether this occurs depends on the variety, weather and the size of the potential crop. Losing some of that potential crop allows the plant to direct its resources to taking the remaining fruit to maturity.

Lateral A branch growing from the main stem.

Layering The practice of using a plant's tendency to grow roots when parts of the plant touch the ground to produce new plants.

Leader The central branch from which laterals will grow, it forms the main stem or trunk at the centre of the plant.

Maiden A tree in the first year after grafting. If it has branches it may be referred to as a 'feathered maiden', if not it may be referred to as a 'maiden whip'.

Minarettes These are essentially cordon trees, grown vertically and not usually attached to wires. They are also known as column, ballerina or leg trees. Minarettes can be planted closely together (perhaps 60cm apart, depending on variety).

Mulch A layer of material primarily used to suppress weeds and minimise water loss from the soil. There is a variety of materials to choose from: mulch mat works well around trees and other large plants as well as over large areas; a 5cm layer of well-rotted manure and/or compost gives a nourishing mulch that releases nutrients over time; and shredded bark, gravel and chippings work well in domestic settings.

Perennial A plant that lives for a number of years.

pH A measure of relative acidity/alkalinity, ranging from 1 (acidic) to 14 (alkaline). Plants may have very specific pH requirements to enable them to thrive.

Pollination Where pollen from the anther reaches the stigma, leading to fertilisation of the flowers and in turn to fruit.

Propagation Creating new plants using material from existing plants, usually by grafting, taking cuttings, layering, using runners, suckers or by dividing them.

Pyramid A tree grown in a pyramid shape (like a Christmas tree), tapering towards the top. A spindlebush is a shorter, squatter version.

Rootstock The lower part of a grafted tree, usually comprising the root system and a short section of the trunk. The rootstock controls the size the plant can grow to, and may be chosen to allow the variety grafted onto it to grow in soils it may otherwise be unable to thrive in.

Runners Stems that usually grow along the surface of the soil, which can root and produce child plants at their end.

Scion A length of fruit wood taken from a parent tree and grafted to a rootstock. It grows into the upper section of the tree and produces fruit of the same variety as the parent.

Self-fertile A plant that is able to pollinate itself.

Spur A short branch or group of branches which bear fruit buds and therefore the flowers and fruit.

Standard A tree with a single clear trunk up to 2m in height. Half-standards are shorter versions.

Stepover A short, trained T-shaped tree (usually a pear or apple), rarely more than 60cm high. In essence, a single-tiered espalier.

Stigma The female part of the flower which receives the pollen from the anther.

Sublateral A shoot growing from a lateral.

Sucker A shoot that grows from the root or rootstock.

Fruit A–Z

All of the well-known fruit that you can grow across most of the country is included in this A–Z. The usual suspects are here – such as pears, plums and apples – as well as a few personal favourites of lesser-known fruit, including Japanese wineberries, which I've included because they're just too good not to be shared.

I grow a lot of marginal fruit here in the Southwest, such as persimmons and pineapple guavas, as the climate is favourable, but for most parts of the country these are not an option so they are not included. Neither are citrus fruit, passion fruit, kiwis or cranberries, because they are unreliable for most, and there are equally delicious and/or more reliable alternatives. That said, I have included some fruit that are far from certainties to produce every year, notably peaches, nectarines and apricots, as they are incredibly satisfying to grow for yourself and in reality you are more likely to get fruit than not. Beyond these few favourites I have drawn a line.

The entries for the different fruit vary in length, but this is no reflection of their deliciousness, nor an indication of their trickiness to grow. Some have particular requirements and it is occasionally vital to give lengthy instructions. Don't be put off by these. You won't find them difficult or time-consuming to follow, it's just that accuracy results in a healthier plant and a bigger harvest.

For each fruit I've included the varieties that have done well for me, that I know to be outstanding or that suit particular requirements such as container growing. There may well be others that are equally delicious or that you may prefer, so be nosy and try to taste the variety you plant before you buy it. If not, trust my suggestions: they're all good.

Pests and diseases that may trouble you are mentioned, and there's a longer description of the main tediums on pp.176–181. Too many growing books start off telling you about the pests and diseases that may come your way – this is a little like the vicar telling you about the rows you will have on the day you get married. You are very likely to come across the odd pest or disease in your garden (as you are likely to have the odd 'frank exchange' with your partner) but it has to be better to celebrate the upside of your partnership rather than meditate on the down. And make no mistake, growing fruit is a partnership – with luck your plants will be with you for some time, so choose well.

Advice on specific growing requirements and harvesting is given under each entry and the chart overleaf provides a guide to overall pruning and harvesting times, so you can see when work needs to be done throughout the year and when you are likely to be gathering the fruit of your labours.

And from the very beginning, remember the point: delicious food to enrich the lives of you and your loved ones. Each fruit includes some ideas for enjoying it, with fuller recipes on pp.192–245.

Pruning and harvesting times

Times for most garden-related tasks vary with the weather, location and aspect, and the varieties you've chosen. Use the following as a guide, rather than a series of deadlines, especially when it comes to harvesting. If the cherries look good but you're unsure whether the timing is right, try one – your taste buds will tell you.

The time to prune is less open to interpretation. Stick with this guide, at least in terms of whether to prune in winter or not, as the timing can greatly influence the likelihood of disease occurring. Prune a plum in winter, for example, and you risk silver leaf far more than if the cuts are made when the sap is rising.

The table doesn't include planting times as there is a simple rule: if your plant is delivered or grown in a pot you can plant it out when you like; if it is bare-root it should be planted between November and March.

	JAN	FEB	MARCH	APRIL	MAY	JUNE	JULY	AUG	SEPT	OCT	NOV	DEC
APPLES												
Pruning	•	•									•	•
Harvest							•	•	•	•		
APRICOTS												
Pruning				•	•							
Harvest							•	•	•			
BLACKBERRIES & HYBRID BERRIES												
Pruning										•	•	•
Harvest							•	•	•			
BLACKCURRANTS												
Pruning	•							•	•	•	•	•
Harvest							•	•				
BLUEBERRIES												
Pruning	•										•	•
Harvest							•	•	•			
CHERRIES												
Pruning				•	•							
Harvest							•	•	•			
FIGS												
Pruning			•	•	•	•						
Harvest								•	•			
GOOSEBERRIES												
Pruning	•						•	•			•	•
Harvest					•	•	•					

	JAN	FEB	MARCH	APRIL	MAY	JUNE	JULY	AUG	SEPT	OCT	NOV	DEC
GRAPES												
Pruning	•					•	•				•	•
Harvest								•	•	•		
JAPANESE WINEBERRIES												
Pruning	•										•	•
Harvest								•	•			
MEDLARS												
Pruning	•										•	•
Harvest										•		
MELONS												
Sowing			•	•								
Harvest								•	•	•		
MULBERRIES												
Pruning			•	•								
Harvest								•	•			
PEACHES & NECTARINES												
Pruning					•	•						
Harvest							•	•	•			
PEARS												
Pruning	•	•									•	•
Harvest								•	•	•	•	
PLUMS, DAMSONS, GAGES ETC.												
Pruning					•	•						
Harvest							•	•	•	•		
QUINCE												
Pruning	•	•									•	•
Harvest										•		
RASPBERRIES												
Pruning		•	•						•	•	•	
Harvest							•	•	•	•	•	
REDCURRANTS & WHITE CURRANTS												
Pruning	•				•	•					•	•
Harvest							•	•				
RHUBARB												
Harvest			•	•	•	•	•					
STRAWBERRIES												
Harvest					•	•	•	•	•	•		

Apple 'Lord Lambourne'

Apples *Malus domestica*

PRUNE	November–February
HARVEST	July–October

Apple trees were probably the first trees grown intentionally for fruit, initially in Turkey, before spreading more widely as people selected better and more fruitful varieties. Tasty, refreshing, nourishing and plentiful at harvest, apples rarely attract birds or wasps and are happy to ripen without a glorious summer. It's easy to see why apples are the most popular fruit tree.

Ordinarily I'd be asking you to consider growing fruit less easy to find in the shops, but all apples are not born the same. There are endless delicious varieties from which to choose but I love the earlies in particular. Ready from midsummer onwards, the early harvested varieties have a fresh liveliness rare in later apples and they're perfect straight off the branch, without the period of storage many later varieties need after picking. 'Beauty of Bath', nipped off the tree in August, are simply astounding. They are at their best only for a short window after picking, which makes them less suitable for the shops. Like mulberries, grapes and the best strawberries, the finest early apples are the preserve of the home grower.

Varieties

With over 7000 varieties to choose from it would be easy to feel overwhelmed by the options and although you'll find only a fraction of those possibilities are easily available, your choice is still a wide one.

I have my own favourites and there are many that are commonly regarded as very fine indeed (see below), but to make the best choice you should ask yourself whether you want apples to eat, cook, make cider or more than one of those.

Cooking apples tend to be larger and more tart than eaters, cider apples are often too harsh for happy eating and dual-purpose varieties may be sharp earlier in the season, mellowing and becoming sweeter as the weeks pass.

Here are a few that I think are outstanding varieties to check out:

Eaters 'Orleans Reinette', 'Beauty of Bath', 'Blenheim Orange', 'Ashmead's Kernel', 'Cox's Orange Pippin' (self-fertile), 'Lord Lambourne', 'Old Somerset Russet'
Cookers 'Bramley', 'Annie Elizabeth'
Ciders 'Kingston Black', 'Browns'
Dual-purpose 'Veitch's Perfection'

If you have limited space to dedicate to growing apples, you should go for a variety that is self-fertile (i.e. it can pollinate itself) otherwise you should ensure that your chosen varieties have flowering periods that at least partially coincide (see p.20). Otherwise a family tree may be for you. These are trees which have two or more varieties grafted onto one main trunk, giving you the opportunity to have different apples on each of the main branches. Approach a fruit nursery direct and they may even be willing to graft the varieties of your choice ready to deliver the following year.

It's also worth considering local varieties as these are likely to flourish where you live. 'Veitch's Perfection' originated a few miles from my home and the trees in my apple orchard grow quickest, produce reliably well and are the healthiest, most round-flavoured apples of the whole orchard. Find yourself a good supplier who'll advise you about any local and delicious cultivars and you will give yourself every chance of fabulous apples and a healthy tree.

There is now an extensive range of rootstocks (see p.126) but the main ones you will find are coded – for example, M27 for a rootstock which produces a dwarfing tree, M106 for a medium-sized tree (around 3m in height) and M25 for a full standard tree. There are many options dependent on site and size, so check with your nursery to find the best for you.

Growing

Apples are as easy to grow as any fruit tree. Although they tend to be happiest as freestanding trees, they do take well to all manner of training – stopovers, cordons, espaliers and even arches – which makes them infinitely adaptable to even the smallest of spaces.

Spacing depends on rootstock and whether and how the tree is being trained (see p.128). For cordons, space your trees 50cm apart, espaliers and stopovers 2m or so apart, and for freestanding trees 3–9m apart (your supplier will give you guidance depending on your rootstock and local conditions).

Whatever the rootstock and whether training or not, plant your tree as outlined on p.146. Mulch around the base, water through extended dry periods in the early years and feed every spring with a good top dressing of well-rotted manure or similar. With a dwarfing rootstock you can grow apples in a large container but the importance of keeping up with feeding and watering greatly increases.

Once formative pruning has taken place (see pp.153–9 for your options), pruning should focus on removing diseased, dead and damaged wood, as well as crossing branches and any congestion in the centre if you're growing your tree as a bush. Prune unwanted branches back flush with the trunk or main branch, but if they're large and likely to leave a long ovate wound, leave them cut as short stubs as this minimises the risk of disease getting in. There are a few options with pruning but for an easy life I'd recommend doing all ongoing apple (and pear) pruning during the dormant winter period between late November and early March.

Spur-bearing

Tip-bearing

The detail of pruning for freestanding trees varies depending whether your variety produces fruit on spurs or the tips of shoots:

Spur-bearing Most apples and pears are of this type, bearing fruit in clusters on spurs (stubby branches) that are at least 2 years old. Cut each lateral back by a third every winter, and each sublateral to five buds to encourage more fruiting buds (and eventually spurs) to develop.

Tip-bearing These trees bear fruit on the tips of last year's growth, so most fruit will be at branch ends rather than along their length. Pruning of tip-bearers involves taking out a quarter of the oldest fruiting branches each year, thereby completely renewing the growth that comes from the main branches every 4 years. Avoid pruning sideshoots and new growth as most fruit will develop here.

Pruning also varies according to any style of training you use (see pp.156–9).

Harvesting and storage

Early apple varieties are ready from late July into September. Eat them immediately as (like early potatoes) they don't keep for long. Most other varieties are ready from October and may need a little storage after picking until they are really at their

Cordon apples

best. Many can be stored for anything up to 6 months. Taste-testing the readiness of these late varieties is tricky. At the right time there should be a few windfall apples at the base of the tree. Pick one from the tree itself and slice it in half – if it's ready the pips should be brown rather than white.

When it comes to picking, take any that give with a gentle, cupped, twisting motion – there should be no sense of pulling as this not only indicates the fruit needs the tree a little longer, but it can also damage fruiting spurs and reduce the following year's crop.

Any apples to be stored should be kept in a dry cool place (such as a garage). Store them in a single layer, not touching each other, ideally on slatted shelving for air circulation, otherwise on newspaper. They should keep for months (depending on seasonality) but check them regularly and remove any that are spoiling.

You can also cook them gently to a pulp and freeze, or cut your apples into rings and dry them in a dehydrator or on the lowest setting of your oven.

Pests and diseases

The legendary caterpillars of fairy tales and nursery rhymes are usually codling moth larvae – just cut out any you see before eating or cooking your apple. If you find them particularly upsetting or your tree appears to be inundated, you can use pheromone traps. These non-chemical traps work by attracting the males, which stick to the trap and hence the females go unmated, halting the life cycle before the caterpillar stage.

Scab (see p.180) can be a pain, and some varieties (such as 'Ashmead's Kernel' and 'Egremont Russet') offer a degree of resistance. Nectria canker (see p.179), a fungal disease, can also be a nuisance.

Eating

Apples combine beautifully with so many partners including black pudding, pork, cabbage and cheese on the savoury side. And most apple varieties take well to cooking, as well as eating raw. Cored whole apples are wonderful baked: stuff them with a cream made by beating equal amounts of butter and sugar together and flavouring with a little ground cinnamon; or try a mincemeat filling.

Peeled, cored and sliced, apples make a wonderful simple compote when slow-cooked with star anise and/or cinnamon, plus a little sugar. Delicious on its own or with yoghurt and granola, the compote can also be used as the fruity part of the cranachan, fool and mess recipes (p.218, p.213 and p.224 respectively).

Recipes Orchard ice cream with caramelised walnuts (p.195) and Blackberry apple compote (p.200). See also variations for fruit leather (p.234), crumble (p.239) and cake (p.232).

Apricot 'Flavourcot'

Apricots *Prunus armeniaca*

PRUNE	May–June
HARVEST	July–September

The Romans developed a taste for apricots after Alexander the Great brought them to Europe, but they didn't quite get to grips with the particularities of growing them in the UK. Others tried in the thirteenth and the sixteenth centuries before they became properly established in the grander homes of the nineteenth century. Until recently you'd rarely see apricots growing anywhere less regal, but they have become increasingly common in gardens and allotments.

The growing interest is at least partly down to the availability of new varieties. Although apricots originate from the warm climes of Armenia, they don't need a spectacular summer to do well here. The fruit are usually ripe by midsummer, even in the northern parts of the country, but the flowers are vulnerable in early spring. Apricots flower early, at the same time as blackthorn, before most of our other fruit blossom dares brave a look, and late frosts can kill off the flowers that would otherwise turn to fruit. New varieties (see below) have been bred to flower later, which, with climate change nudging the last frosts back earlier into the year, really ups your chances of homegrown apricots.

Like peaches, apricots are one of those delights that bear little resemblance to those you buy in shops. Although less luscious than peaches, homegrown apricots have a deeper, richer, muskier flavour than you might be used to. If you can get the flowers past the last frosts you'll find them little troubled by pests and diseases and there's no chance of catching the leaf curl that can deplete other stone fruit.

Varieties

Any of the more recent late-flowering varieties (many of which end in 'cot') are likely to give you the best chance of fresh apricots. 'Flavourcot' ripens just after 'Tomcot', so if you grow them together you'll enjoy a longer picking season.

If you've a sunny, sheltered spot (and are happy to use horticultural fleece to protect the blossom) then do try older varieties such as 'Bredase' and 'Alfred' as, to my mind, they may just pip the newer varieties for depth of flavour.

Apricot trees are usually grafted onto the semi-vigorous 'Torinel' or 'St Julien A' rootstocks, or the semi-dwarfing 'Pixy'.

Look out for new dwarf varieties. I grow 'Champion' which gets to around 1.3m in height and is wonderfully productive for its size.

Apricots are self-fertile so growing a single tree is fine.

Growing

Apricot trees are pretty low maintenance but they do need shelter from harsh winds, and a sunny frost-free spot with a well-drained soil. Neutral to slightly alkaline conditions are best, and avoid sandy or chalky sites.

Plant your tree as described on p.146 and allow at least 4.5m from its neighbour, depending on the rootstock. Apricot trees will happily grow as pyramids, bushes or trained as fans.

Hand pollination with a soft brush will really boost your harvests (see p.189), and even if you grow one of the newer late-flowering varieties it's worth fleecing against late spring frosts that may harm the blossom. Water your tree well through dry periods, especially in the first few years.

Some people thin the fruit, taking out cramped apricots as they develop so that those left on the tree are around 8cm apart, thinking it boosts the viability of the remaining fruit. I tend not to do so, unless the fruit is very obviously touching and overcrowded, as I find the tree naturally jettisons any excess. The choice is yours.

Formative pruning of freestanding apricots follows that of plums (see p.154) and should be done in late spring and summer when the sap is rising to minimise the risk of silver leaf disease (see p.180). Ongoing pruning should be limited to removing dead, diseased and overcrowded branches.

If you are growing your apricot tree as a fan, it should be pruned as described on pp.156–8.

Harvesting and storage

Depending on variety, location and the nature of the summer, apricots can be ready to eat by midsummer even in our unreliable British climate, or as late as early September. Unless you're drying or cooking them, don't try storing apricots. They can be dried in a dehydrator or by placing them in the oven on its lowest setting overnight until they reach the state you require, but they are so much better eaten sun-warm and fresh, straight from the tree, or cooked from fresh.

Pests and diseases

As far as diseases are concerned, bacterial canker (see p.176) and silver leaf (see p.180) are your two main worries.

Birds can wreak havoc with the ripening fruit, although they may not bother them at all – use netting at the first sign of any interest from the birds.

Eating

Fresh from the tree, apricots are a sweet aromatic pleasure and any not eaten in this way are too precious to mess around with too much. Although they make a wonderful jam, I'd avoid preserving too many unless you have a real glut. Enjoy them at their best as they are, or in smoothies or dipped in melted dark chocolate. Or to make a delectable compote, halve, stone and lightly stew apricots – with or without a little cardamom and/or cinnamon. This is delicious with yoghurt, rippled through a flapjack mixture, or used in the fool, cranachan or mess recipes (p.213, p.218 and p.224 respectively).

Recipes Apricots on toast (p.199) and Lamb and apricot tagine (p.196). See also variations for compote (p.200), cake (p.232) and fruit leather (p.234).

Dwarf apricot 'Champion'

Blackberry

Blackberries and hybrid berries
Rubus spp.

PRUNE	October–December
HARVEST	July–September

Whether garden-grown or foraged, blackberries are famously nutritious, being high in fibre, vitamins and minerals. Humans have eaten them for thousands of years, and during the First World War children in England collected blackberries during school time to be juiced and sent to the front line to maintain soldiers' health. Not only fabulous for you, blackberries are easy to grow and happily romp away in almost any soil. So, if you're a beginner, have a less than perfect site, or just fancy some easily acquired and mouthwatering fruit, a homegrown blackberry is definitely for you.

Before anyone gets up in arms, I'm not wanting to put an end to wandering around the hedgerows with a plastic container in search of free fruit – blackberrying is as much a part of summertime as sand castles and ice cream. But many of the domestic varieties are deliciously different to their wild relative and worth growing as well as – rather than instead of – the hedgerow favourites.

Cultivated varieties tend to have fruit that is larger, sweeter and more heavy-cropping than the fruit you forage for. This doesn't make them 'better' – tart can be as delicious as sweet – but where domestic varieties can have the edge is that many are thornless and grow naturally upright, which makes them both pleasant to handle and easier for training.

Of the blackberry hybrids available, tayberries with their gentle acidity to offset the sweetness, along with boysenberries and loganberries with their longer flavour and juiciness, are to my mind the best. Either are worthy of their own spot in the garden on flavour alone, but particularly so as neither fruit is commonly for sale.

Varieties
Of the newer thornless blackberry varieties I've tried, 'Adrienne', 'Helen' (early-fruiting and disease-resistant) and 'Oregon Thornless' are the tastiest. If you'd like to bring the taste of wild blackberries to your garden, then the heavy-cropping 'Ashton Cross' is the one for you.

As far as the hybrids are concerned, tayberries, boysenberries and loganberries are usually sold as generic varieties.

All blackberries and hybrids are self-fertile. Look for certified virus-free plants.

Growing

Blackberries may well be the easiest of all fruit to grow for yourself. They're vigorous and unfussy about site, doing perfectly happily in exposed or shady conditions, or even in heavy soils.

You can let them ramble about for a low-effort harvest or beautify them with support and allow the increased air and sun to give you more fruit into the bargain. If you fancy training them you can just tie them to wires fixed to walls or a shed, or grow them more formally as a fan.

When planting blackberries, cut the strongest stems back to around 30cm, removing any thin shoots to encourage strong shoots to grow. Train strong stems into a fan, tying them across horizontal wires. Snip the ends off when they get to 2m long (or a little less if you're pushed for space), as this encourages lateral shoots to form, which will in turn bear fruit.

Boysenberry

At the end of the harvest, any stems that have produced fruit should be cut right back to the base. This allows new canes to grow and be tied in to the wires, replacing the canes that have fruited.

As with most fruit, blackberries will establish better if you water them well through extended dry periods in the first summer, and if you mulch them around the base every spring with well-rotted organic matter. A watering with comfrey tea or seaweed feed (see p.161) from flowering will boost your crop.

Harvesting and storage

The fruit ripens gradually across the plant from midsummer onwards (depending on the variety) and the best way to test is to pull them gently. When they're ready they will separate easily from the plant, taking the plug with them (raspberries leave it behind when ready). Many of the best new varieties are highly productive – you may get up to 5kg from each plant in a good year. Pick them on a dry day, as wet berries quickly deteriorate. Harvest regularly, as they ripen, to ensure most for you and fewest for the birds.

Blackberries will keep in the fridge for a day or two and freeze very well.

Pests and diseases

Blackberries are fairly trouble-free, although raspberry beetle (see p.109) and birds can deplete your harvest so net them (at least from when the fruit starts to colour) if you can.

Eating

A classic 'one in the basket, one for me' fruit when picking. So deliciously versatile are blackberries you'll find you can adapt all manner of recipes to use them.

And do try blackberry whisky: put 1.5kg blackberries and 250g caster sugar into a large sterilised jar or bottle and pour over a bottle of whisky. The whisky needn't be expensive but it should be a minimum of 40 per cent strength to develop a full flavour. Seal the jar or bottle and, for a month or two, invert the bottle back and forth once a day (on as many days as you remember to). After 3 months, strain the flavoured alcohol into a sterilised bottle and allow the flavour to develop for a year if you can, longer if you have the patience. The result is hard to identify as either part blackberry or whisky, but it is quite superb.

Recipes Blackberry apple compote (p.200), Summer pudding (p.202) and Frozen summer berries and hot white chocolate sauce (p.201). See also variations for cranachan (p.218), mess (p.224), trifle (p.244), granita (p.243), crumble (p.239), clafoutis (p.209), tarts (p.214 and p.240), muffins (p.207), fruit leather (p.234), bottled fruit (p.236) and fruit vodka (p.233).

Blackcurrant 'Ben Hope'

Blackcurrants *Ribes nigrum*

PRUNE	August–January
HARVEST	July–August

Many of us have grown up drinking a rather famous brand of blackcurrant cordial and its popularity probably stems from the Second World War. With our usual overseas supplies of citrus fruit largely blocked by U-boats, the UK was in danger of being starved of vitamin C, so the government encouraged people to grow blackcurrants, which are incredibly high in that essential nutrient. For a few years, from 1942, most of the country's blackcurrants were made into cordial (by the originators of that famous brand) and distributed free as a simple, delicious way of getting vitamin C into the nation's children. And from that moment it's been a familiar part of our lives.

One of the endearing things about blackcurrants is that they are uncomplicated to look after – and you can combine your harvesting with the pruning. As the currants ripen to a deep black you can get in there with the secateurs and snip off the short trusses of fruit or better still chop out the oldest third of the plant right down to the crown with the trusses still attached to the branch. It's the perfect time to cut these branches to the ground to encourage new growth but in doing so you get a good portion of the fruit out without the fiddle. And you can always pick any remaining fruit off the branches.

Put the cut branches into a vase of water at home and you'll have a little longer to use the fruit – just snip or carefully pluck currants off the branch when you're ready to eat them. And don't ignore the leaves (see p.50).

Varieties

There are many blackcurrant varieties to choose from and the 'Ben' cultivars are well worth investigating. They've all been bred to resist frosts and a range of pests and diseases, as well as producing delicious harvests. 'Ben Hope', 'Ben Lomond' and 'Big Ben' (with double-sized berries) have all given hefty harvests of delicious berries for me. 'Ebony' is particularly sweet straight from the bush – and it arrives early, in the first half of July.

Jostaberries are a complicated cross between a gooseberry and a blackcurrant – of a size between the two and tasting more like gooseberries when picked early, and maturing more towards a blackberry flavour. They are delicious, and almost always sold as a generic variety.

Blackcurrants and their crosses are self-fertile.

Growing blackcurrants

Blackcurrants are pleasingly versatile. Happiest in a sunny, fertile location, they'll do perfectly well in a damper spot where most other fruit would complain. Most varieties get to around 1.5m in height and spread, so plant your bush a little more than that distance from its neighbour.

Although they will get by if ignored for a while, blackcurrants will be grateful for watering until they're established and a good mulch of well-rotted manure or compost in spring will be well rewarded. Blackcurrants are hungry and thirsty plants so keep them well fed and watered to get the best from them.

In the first spring after planting, chop the stems down to just above a bud (i.e. almost to the ground). Every year after, you want to chop out around a third of the plant – the oldest parts – to encourage new stems to grow through. You can do this in winter but I prefer to kill a few birds with one stone by doing it at harvest time (see above). Cut as close to the ground as you can.

Blackcurrants can be grown in containers of around 40cm diameter. You'll need to water and feed them very regularly and repot them every 3 years or so.

Harvesting and storage

Blackcurrants are ready to harvest in midsummer. Ripe perfection is quite tough to call – usually it's a little while after the currants turn the deep colour you're expecting. Leave them as long as you can and they'll get even sweeter.

Use a fork to strip the currants from the trusses.

Pests and diseases

Birds seem to know exactly when the fruit is perfectly ripe and will leave it entirely undisturbed until that moment. Having lulled you into a false sense of security, they can decimate your crop in no time, so do net your plants as they ripen.

Gall midge maggots and blister aphids love young blackcurrant leaves. Pick off and incinerate any leaves that discolour or distort.

Bud mites can inhabit the buds, making them fat and rounded instead of long and thin. It's easy to spot their effect in spring as growth begins. Cut off any affected stems.

Eating

Small, tart-sweet and intense blackcurrants are perhaps best used almost as herbs, where their flavour rather than their substance is what matters. Ice cream, granita, jam, curd, sauce and jelly are all wonderful vehicles for full-flavoured blackcurrants to shine.

And do try the leaves: not only do they make a refreshing tea (and I'm no fan of most fruit teas), but blackcurrant leaf sorbet is particularly fine. It is also comforting to have a recipe for the leaves if the birds have beaten you to any unnetted currants. Dissolve 140g caster sugar in 220ml boiling water. Throw in a generous handful of blackcurrant leaves and take off the heat. Once completely cool, strain and add the juice and finely grated zest of 2 lemons, then pour into a large, shallow plastic container. Freeze until almost firm, then scratch up thoroughly with a fork and incorporate a lightly beaten egg white. Freeze until solid.

Recipes Frozen summer berries and hot white chocolate sauce (p.201), Summer pudding (p.202) and Crème de cassis (p.204). See also variations for fruit leather (p.234), compote (p.200), granita (p.243), fool (p.213), muffins (p.207), clafoutis (p.209), tart (p.214) and cake (p.232).

Blueberry 'Bluecrop'

Blueberries *Vaccinium* spp.

PRUNE	November–January
HARVEST	July–September

If you like your fruit sweet with a little balancing sharpness, and perfect to eat when plucked straight from the plant, blueberries are for you. They look like a flashy blackcurrant – a little larger and dusted with icing sugar. Their flavour lives up to their looks and they're well worth the particular care they need.

Native to North America, blueberries came to the UK in 1949, imported by the Trehane family who still run the Dorset Blueberry Company, growing the fruit and selling excellent blueberry plants. There aren't endless blueberry farms dotted across the countryside for one main reason: blueberries need acidic soil, anything else just won't do. We don't produce many for the domestic market, yet demand is ever-increasing. It keeps the price of blueberries high in the shops, and gives you another fine reason to grow them.

They are as beautiful as they are tasty. Check out the base of the fruit where the blossom formed, away from the stem. This lazily lobed five-pointed star on each fruit was seen by some Native Americans as a sign that the Great Spirit had sent 'starberries' to ease hunger in times of famine. They are also famously nutritious, full of vitamins and minerals, and reputed to have beneficial effects on anything from heart disease to depression. Whether they are or not, they make a mighty fine muffin, so they get my vote.

Varieties

There are plenty of fabulous, prolific fruiters out there: 'Sunshine Blue', 'Bluecrop' and 'Chandler' are all excellent, but do go to a specialist provider to make sure you get the best plants. They are partially self-fertile, which in theory at least means one plant should produce some fruit but in practice they do poorly – I've found that three bushes or more will give me all the blueberries I need and ensure good pollination.

Look for certified disease-free plants, or propagate your own (using softwood cuttings, see p.131) from healthy plants.

Growing

It is very easy to coax a heavy, reliable harvest from blueberries if you give them the right conditions. They will only thrive in a rich acidic soil (ideally pH 5.5 or lower), which has good drainage. You'll need to water your plants with rainwater as tap

Blueberry 'General' in flower

water tends to be alkaline and ongoing watering will gradually neutralise the compost and productivity will slide. The same applies with mulching – use acidic material such as shredded bark or pine needles. Given their particular requirements, blueberries are the perfect candidates for container growing (using an ericaceous compost), where it tends to be easier to maintain the ideal pH.

Blueberries do like light and heat, so give them a sheltered spot with as much summer sun as you can. Plant them at least 1.5m or so from their neighbour.

Use a lime-free fertiliser to boost soil nutrient levels without compromising the pH.

Do your pruning in the winter, taking out any damaged or dead shoots and about a quarter of the dominant shoots. Also cut back by half any weaker shoots to encourage strong growth each year.

Harvesting and storage

With a spread of varieties you can be eating fresh blueberries from midsummer through to autumn. Blueberries fruit on wood that's up to 3 years old, ripening to their talcy-blue colour from midsummer onwards. The berries ripen gradually across the plant rather than all at once, so you need take only those that have reached perfect ripeness each time. Be patient and let them develop a deep indigo colour – as they do so their flavour is getting better and better.

Blueberries should keep for a couple of weeks in the fridge but the flavour can deteriorate fairly quickly. In practice you'll be lucky to get many as far as the kitchen, they taste so good straight off the bush, but any surplus can be frozen.

Pests and diseases

Blueberries are remarkably trouble-free, other than the birds, which can be netted against if they become a nuisance.

Eating

Much of the flavour of blueberries comes from their skin so they don't take as well to sauces and the like as blackcurrants. They're better kept whole rather than stewed, although cooking does bring out their flavour. Get them into anything that's baked and they shine – muffins, tarts, cakes, pancakes and puddings.

Recipes Blueberry muffins (p.207) and Frozen summer berries and hot white chocolate sauce (p.201). See also variations for cranachan (p.218), clafoutis (p.209), tart (p.214), summer pudding (p.202), fruity melons (p.223) and compote (p.200).

Cherry 'Morello'

Cherries *Prunus avium* and *Prunus cerasus*

PRUNE	May–June
HARVEST	July–September

The cherry matches the sublime flavour of its fruit with its looks for much of the year, more so than any other fruit tree. Littered with early blousy blossom in spring, hanging with juicy earrings through summer, followed by classic autumn leaves, cherries are as good value as you can get from a tree. We used to grow them in vast numbers in the UK but the manpower shortages during the world wars started a slide that was exacerbated by cheap imports, to such a degree that we've lost 95 per cent of our cherry orchards in 60 years. On the upside, over the last few decades plant breeders have succeeded in developing smaller self-fertile trees, ideal for either back gardens or commercial orchards, dispensing with the need for huge ladders and endlessly extending loppers.

There are sweet (*Prunus avium*) and sour or acid (*Prunus cerasus*) cherries, and I'd urge you to look as long and hard at the sour as the sweet when making your choice. The prince of the sour cherries is the 'Morello' – for 400 years it's had few contenders for its crown. Sours are twice as laden with vitamin C as sweet varieties and will happily fruit on a north- or east-facing wall.

If you fancy the sweet cherries, and why not, then you'll be battling with our feathered friends (*avium* means 'for the birds') so be prepared to net your trees, as they'll decimate them in the time it takes to load your blunderbuss.

Varieties

The 'Morello' is hard to rival if you're after a sour cherry, and the trees are self-fertile so growing just one is fine.

There are many fabulous sweet varieties to choose from, so I can do little more than recommend the ones I've found best, while steering you towards nurseries (such as Thornhayes, see Directory, p.248) who know their cherries and those that might suit your location well. 'Lapins', 'Stella' and 'Summer Sun' are as good as any of the newer self-fertile varieties, and if you fancy your chances of growing one without netting, then the white-cherried 'Vega' is the one for you.

You may still find the odd nursery selling trees that are crosses between sour and sweet cherries. These are known as 'Dukes', and their name often gives that away; 'May Duke' is one example.

Modern varieties on dwarfing rootstocks (like 'Gisela') can be kept to a couple of metres in height, but allow 3–4m if you want to train them into a fan.

If you are growing varieties which are not self-fertile, make sure that their pollination groups are compatible. These are usually numbered or lettered, as for apples and pears, and should be either the same or adjacent.

Most cherries are grafted onto 'Colt' (semi-vigorous, 4–5m height) or 'Gisela 5' (dwarfing, 2–3m height).

Growing

Sweet cherries love full sun, whereas sour cherries make a perfect choice for shady spots, especially north- or east-facing walls. The blossom tends to come early and can be susceptible to frost damage, so give them a sheltered position and keep horticultural fleece to hand as a nocturnal duvet – but do remove it early in the morning to allow pollination to occur.

Cherries need a good deep, fertile, well-drained soil. You should avoid a site that ever becomes waterlogged, but they do like a reasonable amount of water and their shallow roots make them susceptible to drying out fairly quickly. Water them well through dry periods, especially in the early years. A good ring of compost and slow-release fertiliser in late winter will help keep the upper layers of soil fertile for these shallow-rooting trees.

Very dwarfing rootstocks mean you can plant trees as close as 2.5m from each other, or over 6m for full-sized trees.

Cherries can be grown as bushes and pyramids but, given their delicate blossom and the attention of birds, training (as a minarette or fan) is an attractive option for cherries. That said, if you can give a freestanding cherry protection from harsh winds and frosts, little beats the sight of one in full blossom in spring.

Pruning and training freestanding sweet cherries is as for plums (see p.154). Ideally, you should choose a plant with a good goblet shape. And, because they fruit in clusters at the base of year-old stems and on older wood, limit pruning of freestanding cherries to taking out dead, diseased or crossing branches after harvesting. Silver leaf (see p.180) loves cherry trees and pruning cuts are the easiest way in for it, though this is minimised in the warmer months with the sap rising.

Freestanding sour cherries are pruned as for sweet varieties until the third year. Sour varieties crop along the length of stems that grew the previous year so, whether you're growing yours in a fan or freestanding, chop out a good amount of the older wood as this is unproductive, and removing it encourages new growth that will fruit the following year. If you're hoping to grow your cherry as a fan then I'd advise you to buy one already partially trained, otherwise follow the formative training as for plums (see pp.156–8).

Sweet cherry fans need ongoing pruning in early summer to maintain their shape. Any growth pointing towards the wall or outwards can be snipped off, as can some of the older unproductive growth where there are strong newer shoots to be tied in to replace it. Snip back new shoots to 8cm to direct energies to ripening fruit. Sour cherries grown as fans need more pruning than sweet varieties: in summer prune out older branches, tying in new growth which will then produce fruit the next year.

Cherries naturally thin their fruit, dropping any excess they feel incapable of taking to ripeness, so you won't need to do any thinning out early on.

Unless you're growing white cherries, have some netting to hand once the fruit begins to colour to deter birds, which are capable of decimating a crop in no time.

Cherries on dwarfing rootstocks can be grown in pots but you'll need to keep right on top of watering and feeding to stop them struggling.

Harvesting and storage

Most cherries will be ready to eat in the second half of summer. Pick them by the stalks in dry weather, taking care to avoid bruising the delicate fruit. Cherries may keep in the fridge for up to a fortnight but the flavour of sweet varieties may decline in the cold – it's best to eat these as soon as you can. Sour cherries are too harsh to eat raw unless you get them perfectly ripe, but cooked they are stupendous.

Pests and diseases

Bacterial canker (see p.176) and silver leaf (see p.180) are the main culprits, and you may find blackfly at the tips of new shoots, which can be wiped off quite easily. Blossom wilt (see p.176), phytophtera (see p.179) and shothole (see p.180) can trouble your cherry too.

Eating

Cherries are a precious crop. If you've managed to get them past the birds' attentions you'll want to enjoy each and every one. Sweet cherries are irresistible fresh from the tree. And they are excellent in salads with lively leaves such as rocket, and with goat's cheese and hazelnuts or walnuts.

Sour cherries are usually best cooked. A compote of sour cherries with hot smoked sea trout is one of my favourite of Hugh's recipes: gently cook the halved, stoned cherries in a pan with 1 tbsp water and around a fifth of the cherries' weight in light brown sugar. You can always add a little more sugar when the cherries have broken down to form a compote but they should still be a little tart.

Cherries and chocolate is one of the finest combinations – try finishing the clafoutis with a dusting of cocoa. The stones carry more than a hint of almond, so leave the stones in when cooking cherries if you want to enhance the flavour.

Recipes Clafoutis (p.209) and Fruity melons (p.223). See also variations for bottled fruit (p.236), pear and rocket salad (p.228), tart (p.214) and cake (p.232).

Fig 'White Marseilles'

Figs *Ficus carica*

PRUNE	April–July
HARVEST	August–September

Figs are one of those 'fruits' that's not really a fruit, as any resident of Pedants' Corner will rejoice in reminding us. Each of those delicious bulbous knobbles is an extraordinary capsule of tiny flowers, which somehow, in the absence of light, bloom and develop seeds while hidden away. Sink your teeth into that luscious sweet flesh and you're sucking up a soup of yesterday's flowers, and there are few fruity flavours to touch it.

Figs have a reputation for being tricky to care for and trickier to coax a harvest out of, but, as with many fruits, get a few things right and choose the best varieties and you'll give yourself every chance of success.

They need a cracking position with plenty of sun and shelter if you want to get a good harvest of well-ripened fruit – and full ripeness is critical to enjoying the full, deep, luscious flavour of a fig. At their peak, the aromatics tell you the fruit is ready. At this point figs may be very delicate and difficult to handle – far beyond being suitable for transporting to the supermarkets. They can be good if you buy them close to the place they were grown, but this is why nothing beats your own. The telltale sign is a sweet honey tear in the eye of the fig – when you see that, you're in.

Varieties

Although wild figs are pollinated by a wasp that enters the fruit, domestic cultivars are almost without exception self-fertile. Figs come in varieties that bear brown-purple fruit or white-green fruit, which is often given away in the variety name. 'Brown Turkey' is probably the most widely available of any and, although delicious and reliable, it can be a little ordinary in a less-than-sunny summer. 'Petite Nigra', as its name suggests, produces small dark figs which are as good as any for flavour. It's also the one that seems happiest growing in a pot.

'Rouge de Bordeaux', with its small purple fruits and ruby-coloured flesh, is a delicious variety that ripens reliably both under cover and in sheltered, sunny spots outside.

Although marginally less reliable than 'Brown Turkey', I prefer the flavourful sweetness of 'White Marseilles'. It can get rust on the leaves, which is usually only cosmetic, but the taste makes it worth a little occasional shabbiness. 'Excel' is another excellent new white fig.

Growing

Contrary to the common view, figs are easy, low-maintenance plants but they are very particular about a few things. If you're growing them outside they will do best against (or near) a south-facing wall to maximise the light and heat they receive. They need a fertile humus-rich, well-drained soil (or compost if grown in a pot) and some restriction placed on their root system.

If allowed to grow freely, the roots will spread and encourage green growth rather than fruiting so it's best to plant them in a large container (70cm or so in diameter) or restrict their root growth in the ground. You can buy root-restricting bags (from Reads or other suppliers, see Directory, pp.248–9) or create a box (70cm square and deep) with paving slabs or similar. This should reduce their spread from up to 3m high and wide to around half that.

An early spring mulch of composted horse manure or a slow-release organic fertiliser will give them a real boost, and fortnightly liquid feeds of comfrey or seaweed will encourage productivity. Avoid nitrogen-rich feeds (such as nettle tea) as these will encourage green growth over fruiting. Water figs regularly through the summer: this should be daily during dry periods or if you're growing your plant in a container.

Refresh the top 3–4cm of compost for any container-grown figs every spring, and pot them into a larger pot every 4 years or so, but not too often as they fruit particularly well when slightly pot-bound.

Figs can be grown as bushes, half-standards or trained into fans.

For freestanding trees, look for a tree with a well-established goblet framework of five or so branches from a central stem. Every spring prune out any dead, diseased or crossing branches and remove any branch that may be trying to form a new central leader. If there are a few long laterals that are fruiting only at their tips you can prune them back to a bud around 8cm from the trunk or branch to encourage new growth, but do bear in mind when pruning that new fruit will develop near the end of young shoots. In the summer, you can also prune off the growing tip of new shoots once six leaves have appeared – this directs energies to producing the second burst of young fruit.

If you intend to grow figs in a fan, I would recommend buying an established one, as this will save much early grief. Otherwise train your young plant initially as outlined on pp.156–8, spacing the branches well apart as the leaves are large and will shade the fruit if grown too closely together. Once established, aim to remove around a quarter of the oldest branches each spring to reduce congestion and stimulate new growth. In midsummer remove any buds or shoots that are growing into or out from the wall or fence, and prune out any growth that is shading the developing fruit. Tie in any new growth that will add to the main framework of the fan.

Do wear gloves when pruning as the sap can irritate your skin. It also helps to prune from low to high on the plant, to avoid being dripped on.

Plants can produce new young figs twice a year – once in spring and later in summer. This means the plants will often have fruit of different sizes as summer comes to a close: large almost-ripe figs, tiny fruit (pea-sized and smaller, some of which may be tucked into a joint between leaf and stem), and those in between. The large ones will soon be ready to eat, the small ones are next year's fruit and the ones in between should be removed. They won't ripen this year and are likely to toughen over winter, split and weaken the plant, which can impair the ripening of further fruit. Be ruthless: snip them off every November.

If your plant is in a pot, move it under cover for the winter if you can, otherwise insulating with horticultural fleece, bubble wrap and/or straw will do much to nurse your fig through the cold months.

Harvesting and storage

Figs are best eaten straight from the tree, in the late-summer sun. Most varieties ripen a handful every day over a period of a couple of weeks or so, the centre turning tacky and moist with the eye at the base opening a little. This eye may even weep a sugary tear – the perfect time to pick. The longer you can leave it before you pick, the sweeter your reward.

If (and it's a big if) you don't devour your figs sun-warm from the tree, you can preserve them by drying gently in a low oven (55°C) overnight, keeping the dried figs in the fridge until you eat them.

Pests and diseases

Coral spot (see p.178) is the only nuisance other than birds and wasps for outdoor figs, but you will need to watch for red spider mite (see p.179) and brown scale (see p.177) for those grown under cover.

Eating

Ripeness is the critical factor with figs – their perfume develops late and embellishes the flavour beautifully. For the most part it's best to keep it simple with figs – focusing on combinations that bring out their best. Saltiness and nuts are wonderful partners – blue cheese, prosciutto, walnuts and hazelnuts in particular.

Recipes Baked figs with honey and cardamom (p.210). See also variations for bottled fruit (p.236) and pear and rocket salad (p.228).

Gooseberries *Ribes uva-crispa*

PRUNE	July–August, November–January
HARVEST	May–July

Getting together once a year to see who's got the largest gooseberries may seem little more than a harmless, peculiarly male, British pastime, but for over 200 years this is exactly what's been happening every second Tuesday in August in Egton Bridge, Yorkshire. Thank goodness it has been. Once one of a hundred or more gooseberry shows, the Egton Bridge get-together has sown a 200-year thread from a time when gooseberries enjoyed huge popularity, through the leaner periods, to the current beginnings of a resurgence.

Dips in popularity were mainly due to our obsession with sweetness. A tax on sugar in the nineteenth century saw a huge decline in soft-fruit growing, especially those fruit on the sharper side. And in the latter part of the twentieth century, as our tastes became ever sweeter, they appeared less and less in allotments and back gardens. Now they're back on the up, as more of us have learnt to love their early-season sharpness and the fragrant sweetness of those harvested later in the summer. And for that we should be grateful to those who kept the candle burning.

Varieties

Gooseberries are self-fertile, so growing just one plant is fine. Although a slightly untidy division, gooseberries are usually sold as either cooking or dessert varieties. The latter is supposed to indicate that when fully ripe the berries are sweet enough to eat fresh from the bush, but in practice many of the cookers sweeten considerably if left on the plant to develop longer. 'Leveller' has been around for over 150 years and is the one I'd recommend for the half-and-half harvest, as it produces heavy crops of large golden-green berries. These are gorgeous taken sharp and early, leaving some to grow on into sweet, delicious late-season gooseberries.

'Hinnomaki Red' is one of my favourite sweeter varieties, producing a good crop of big, sweet deep-red/purple berries, while being pretty resistant to mildew.

Growing

Although very hardy, gooseberries love sun and shelter, and growing in a moist but well-drained fertile soil. It's best to avoid shallow sandy soils, which tend to be dry and encourage mildew. Gooseberries will still throw out a good (if reduced) harvest in a shady position, and are worth considering if you have a north-facing wall in need of trained fruit.

Gooseberry 'Hinnomaki Red'

Gooseberries are most commonly grown as bushes, pruned into an open goblet on a short trunk. They also take well to being grown with a taller trunk as a standard, or as a cordon. This last option involves growing the plant as a single tall, narrow stem. It produces excellent harvests for its size and is perfect for those with limited space. Gooseberries can also be fan-trained against a wall and/or wire supports. Position your plants around 90cm from each other, or half as much if grown as cordons.

Watering through dry periods will help good fruit development, and it is essential in the first year as the plant gets established. Gooseberries love potassium (comfrey or seaweed feed is a particularly good source) as it encourages healthy fruiting while reducing the likelihood of mildew. Spraying or watering every fortnight from mid-spring through summer is ideal.

Gooseberries appear on short spurs growing from laterals that are 2 or 3 years old. Older laterals produce very few, so the aim is to have a plant with laterals between 1 and 3 years old.

As soon as you plant your gooseberry, prune off any laterals lower than 20cm up the trunk; this gives a clear 'leg' of the goblet shape you are aiming for. Choose the six (at most) best, well-spaced laterals to form your main framework. Cut these back by half to an outward-facing bud and prune any other laterals off completely.

Next winter, prune back the new growth on the six laterals by half. Also prune back any new growth in the centre of the plant or towards the ground to just a single bud; this encourages fruiting spurs to develop.

In subsequent years, first do as you should with any pruning: clip out dead or diseased branches, and any shoots growing out of the main trunk. Any crossing branches or those in congested areas should be cut back to around 2cm long. Prune off old, unproductive laterals, shortening those that remain by a quarter to an inward-facing bud, to retain the upright shape of the plant. If what remains is still slightly overcrowded, then don't be afraid to thin out some of the new growth a little. Cutting out the old material keeps the plant lively and productive, while an open centre allows light and air to get in, keeping disease to a minimum and encouraging good fruiting. In early summer, brave the sharpness of the prickles and prune back the sublaterals to five leaves or so.

If you fancy growing a gooseberry as a cordon, immediately after planting choose one strong branch as your vertical leader and tie this to a cane. Cut off any shoots lower than 15cm above the ground and prune the rest down to one or two buds. The following summer, prune back new growth to five leaves or so and keep tying in the vertical leader. The following winter, shorten the leader by around a third, and snip back that year's growth to one or two buds. As ever, prune anything that's dead, diseased or damaged, and any congested areas should be thinned to allow light and air in.

Continue this cycle of pruning every year, keeping the leader snipped back to the desired height, and you'll have a healthy gooseberry harvest from virtually no ground space.

Harvesting and storage

I like to pick gooseberries in two main instalments: half when they're not fully ripe in late spring/early summer when the elderflower is still about, leaving the rest to ripen further for picking later in the summer, when they'll be much sweeter than the early tart fruit. Some varieties have the potential to become naturally sweeter than others (see above) and if the plant and the summer looks like it's going well, I occasionally leave the lot to develop.

Wear gloves – the thorns are unforgiving.

Pests and diseases

American mildew can form on young shoots, leaves and fruit, especially in crowded plants where air circulation is poor. Resistant varieties are available, although the likelihood of getting mildew is greatly reduced by hard pruning and good air circulation. If it turns up, wipe off the powdery bloom and prune any affected shoots once you've harvested the fruit.

Sawfly caterpillars are only 2cm long but can strip leaves in a very short time, wiping the plant out if left unchecked, so keep a close eye on the plants and pick off any caterpillars you spot immediately.

Birds can be a nuisance, especially with the sweeter berries, so do net your plants if you're not willing to share more than a few.

Eating

Gooseberries are as generous as it gets: prolific and offering an early sharp/sour harvest followed by a sweet picking later in summer. Although just topped and tailed they can star in tarts and crumbles, a gentle stewing gives you the base to create a sharp sauce that's wonderful with oily and/or smoked fish, or to use in dessert recipes.

Recipes Gooseberry fool with elderflower (p.213), Gooseberry curd (p.216) and Gooseberry tart (p.214). See also variations for crumble (p.239), cake (p.232), mess (p.224), cranachan (p.218), compote (p.200) and granita (p.243).

Grapes *Vitis vinifera*

PRUNE	June–July, November–January
HARVEST	August–October

Years ago I went grape picking in France and Switzerland. It was hard work, but the countryside was incredible, the air fresh and we were offered huge meals. Six times a day, starting at 9.30am (a couple of hours into the working day), we were offered chocolate and wine. The sense of celebration at the harvest stuck with me. We don't seem to have that so much in this country any more but now I've planted a small vineyard of my own I'm determined to recreate it. I hope you will too, even if you only plant one or two vines for making wine or for eating the grapes.

Few plants are so devoted to the sun. Every extra moment of sunshine that hits your grapes adds another degree of sweetness to their flavour, and many won't reach perfection until mid-autumn. Unfortunately this leaves your harvest a hostage to the weather. One year you may be snipping off huge, healthy bunches, the next cursing the late frosts or the lack of late summer sun. Take heart: there is a vineyard in Scotland, and with the right choice of varieties and the relative shelter of your garden or allotment, you should get fruit more summers than not. It's well worth it as grapes eaten fresh from your own vine (or turned into wine) are very special.

Even if you're short of space, grapes are one fruit you should still be able to find room for. Growing them vertically means they take up little ground space, and as long as you keep nutrients and water topped up they'll produce perfectly happily grown in large pots.

Varieties

'Solaris' and 'Phoenix' are two excellent white varieties to grow if you want to have grapes for both eating and wine-making.

'Muscat of Alexandria' has a wonderful muscat flavour and aroma, but its oval berries need a little protection to get them fully ripe.

'Regent' is a vigorous, disease-resistant variety producing very large, sweet, blue-black grapes. It is great for winemaking and eating fresh, and its beautiful red autumn foliage adds end-of-season colour to the garden. 'Black Hamburg' is another delicious black grape variety, often producing enormous bunches, but it does need the very sunniest site or to be grown under cover.

'Madeleine Angevine' is a sweet white grape, ideal for anyone wanting to make wine further up-country, as it flowers late, missing the frosts, and ripens early.

Grapes are self-fertile.

Grape 'Seyval Blanc'

Growing

Grapes love sun and warmth, so give them as much as you can. Plant them in a free-draining soil, shelter them from cold winds and late spring frosts and you'll have a good chance of healthy plentiful bunches.

It's hard to beat a south-facing wall, where the extra heat and shelter will tip the odds of ripe fruit in your favour. For support and to guide growth, you'll want a pair of horizontal galvanised wires at least 15cm from the wall, 35cm or so apart, with the lowest 40cm or so above the ground, fixed with vine eyes drilled into the wall or posts.

If you're growing vines in a row, align them north to south so that the sunlight reaches both sides of the plants equally.

However you're growing your vine, planting is the same. In late autumn or early spring dig down to at least 50cm to ensure you give your plant good drainage. Add well-rotted manure or compost and dig it into the base of the hole along with a few handfuls of grit or gravel. Plant the grape to the same depth as it was in the pot, backfilling with the soil you dug out.

Although grapes will usually be perfectly OK without, a good 10cm layer of well-rotted manure or compost around (but not touching) the base of the plant will act as a nourishing, weed-suppressing mulch. And from flowering through fruiting, a fortnightly feed with seaweed or comfrey liquid will give the plant extra potassium, which will boost the health and size of your crop.

Sunlight is the key to perfectly ripe grapes – tear off any leaves shading the bunches. Watering through extended dry periods will improve your chances of fruit. Keep a particular eye out if you are growing your vine near a wall as it is likely to dry out more quickly.

As long as you keep up with the watering and feeding, grapes can be grown perfectly well in containers with a minimum 30cm diameter. And there's the advantage that you can take them indoors through the coldest months.

Don't be intimidated by what can seem like a bit of a pruning palaver with grapes. There are endless methods for training vines formally along a line and the 'Double Guyot' is as good as any, but for most people, growing grapes under cover, in a container or small space or up and over a pergola are more likely options, and for this you should proceed as follows:

Fix three horizontal wires 45cm apart and with the lowest 45cm above the soil. After planting your vine, push a bamboo cane into the soil by the vine and tie it in to the wires vertically. As the shoots begin to grow, choose the strongest and train it up the cane, rubbing or pruning off the others, including any sideshoots that try to grow. The following winter cut the main stem down to just below the top wire.

The next spring/summer choose the strongest shoot at the top of the main stem to grow, pinching off any others. Choose three shoots along either side of the main

Training a grapevine

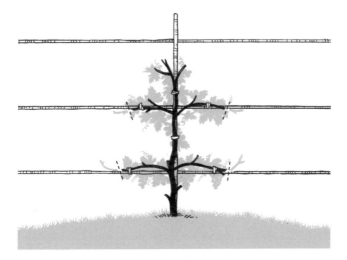

Second summer: Tie in laterals, prune at 30cm, and pinch off the top of the vertical shoot from the main stem.

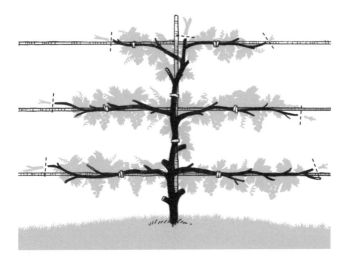

Third summer: Prune off lateral tips three leaves beyond the second bunch of grapes. Rub off shoots growing from the top of the main stem.

stem that are best placed to be trained along the three horizontal wires and tie them in loosely to the wires. Prune off any other sideshoots. When these sideshoots (known as laterals) reach 30cm or so, snip or pinch off the growing tips, and do the same with the vertical shoot from the main stem. You can let two or three bunches develop this year but no more – allow the plant to use most of its energy to establish itself. Remove any others that try to develop when they are tiny.

The following winter, prune back the main stem to just below the top wire and snip back the sideshoots to short spurs of three buds.

In spring/summer, these buds will start to grow. Choose the strongest new sideshoot from each spur, and as it grows tie it along the wire, pruning off any other sideshoots. These sideshoots will produce bunches of grapes – you should allow a maximum of two bunches per sideshoot. Pinch off the end of each sideshoot three leaves beyond its second bunch of grapes – this focuses the plant's energies on producing fruit rather than growing further outwards. Prune off any shoots trying to grow from the top of the main stem.

In subsequent years you can follow the same process as for this third year, although you should be able to allow three bunches per sideshoot.

If you are letting your grape ramble over a pergola or other object, just concentrate on training the main stem up to the required height, tying it in loosely to give it support. After a couple of years a woody framework will have formed and your vine will begin to produce flowers, and then grapes. You can adopt the system described above perfectly well for pergolas too. For a year or two it's worth pinching out the weakest bunches when they're small, leaving four bunches per vine. This isn't essential but it will allow the four to develop fully and means the plant gets enough resources to establish too. From mid-December and before the end of January, thin out overcrowded growth and prune back any areas that are outgrowing the space you have for it.

As with most fruit grown in containers, keep up with watering and ensure the nutrients are topped up with manure, compost and liquid feeds.

Harvesting and storage

Harvest timing varies with variety, the sunniness (or otherwise) of the summer and location, but you may be eating your grapes any time between mid-August and the end of October. Although most grapes approaching ripeness become softer (and in the case of white grapes, more glassy and opaque), tasting the odd grape is really the best way of ascertaining the right moment to pick. Leave the fruit to develop as long as you dare, and snip the whole bunch off when you pick.

Grapes will keep for up to a fortnight in the fridge, depending on the variety and ripeness.

Pests and diseases

Downy and powdery mildews (see pp.178 and 179) can be a problem in damp years. Ventilation and good air circulation is vital – a gentle wind is the best fungicide there is. But should either of these mildews become evident, a sulphur-based spray (see Directory for suppliers, pp.248–9) will help minimise damage.

Birds and wasps can be a nuisance to varying degrees from year to year. Netting and wasp traps are your best remedy.

Eating

You'll not find grapes in too many recipes – they tend not to take well to cooking. They are lovely with cheese, nuts and spicy leaves, such as mizuna and rocket, of course, but if you ask me, you may as well just revel in the pleasure of your own grapes eaten fresh from the vine.

Recipes Chicken Véronique (p.217) and Fruity melons (p.223).

Japanese wineberry

Japanese wineberries
Rubus phoenicolasius

PRUNE	November–January
HARVEST	August–September

Japanese wineberries are one of my very favourite fruit and an absolute must for even the smallest garden.

Although related to raspberries, Japanese wineberries are not a hybrid. They were brought to Europe and North America from their native China, Korea and Japan to cross with raspberries, but their taste stands up on its own. While there is a superficial similarity with raspberries, the flavour of wineberries is longer and has a winey depth like that of well-ripened grapes.

They'll be equally happy grown formally or left ramshackle: you can allow their long, hairy plum-red canes to clamber around as they like, or train them into a strict fan. These long canes throw out sideshoots with large clusters of small pale-pink flowers in early summer that turn into succulent, unbelievably sweet berries, which develop within a papery covering (the calyx). This protects the berries as they grow, peeling open only as the fruit nears maturity. Looking like small raspberries, they poke out green, before traffic-lighting through yellow, orange, and into ripe deep-red over a day or two. This gives the birds little warning and means you get the lot with almost no competition.

After picking, as the colder weather arrives, you get to enjoy the colour of their arching leafless canes as a reminder of the fruit that's gone and is to come.

Varieties

Japanese wineberries are almost always sold as a generic variety.

Growing

Japanese wineberries are self-fertile so having only one plant is fine. While you can grow them from seed, they're rarely available, so start with a plant and you'll also be that much nearer to delicious fruit. If you know someone who has a Japanese wineberry or you want to expand your numbers, you can take advantage of their ability to spread by rooting. All you need to do is encourage the tip of a wineberry cane into the ground and it will form roots. Cut this free from the main plant 30cm or so above the new roots once they are well formed and you have a new plant. You can take hardwood cuttings (see p.130) in late autumn too.

Japanese wineberries pretty much take care of themselves. They are equally at home in a shady spot or a sunny one, and will survive in most soils, but give them a sheltered position with a moist, well-drained soil and they'll fruit prolifically.

You can allow them to scramble about as they like, train them tightly into fans or somewhere in between. Mine are loosely tied to a wire fence, which gives them enough opportunity to ramble but with some sense of order. I have a walnut tree I'm thinking of growing one through too – they fruit equally happily however you grow them.

The furry canes often grow over 2m in length in the first year but grow no longer the following year. Instead, sideshoots with small leaves begin to pop out along the length of each cane, followed by flowers on the ends of the sideshoots in late spring/early summer. These form the fruit.

Pruning is simple. Snip out the canes that have fruited (the ones with old crusty calyxes) any time from autumn onwards but I leave it until late winter, so I can enjoy the fuzzy plum-coloured canes in the winter sunshine.

Harvesting and storage

Japanese wineberries' lack of thorns makes picking them a treat, and the timing of the harvest couldn't be better – filling the lull between the peak of the summer and autumn raspberries, so I get to keep eating Eton mess without a break.

The fruit ripens slowly across the plant rather than in one go, so you're likely to have at least a fortnight of gentle harvesting. Let them get deeply red before you pick, to allow the flavour to develop fully – it's worth the wait.

Pests and diseases

I've never known a wineberry suffer from any diseases, and their magical ability to cover their fruit until they're almost ready means the pests get little chance to get in before you.

Eating

Picked at perfect ripeness, Japanese wineberries are easily polished off way before they make it to your kitchen. If you decide to cook with them don't lose them in a mix of berries – let their individuality come through on its own.

Recipes Cranachan (p.218) and Frozen summer berries with hot white chocolate sauce (p.201). See also variations for mess (p.224), fool (p.213), compote (p.200), bottled fruit (p.236), vodka (p.233), granita (p.243) and fruit leather (p.234).

Medlar 'Nottingham'

Medlars *Mespilus germanica*

PRUNE	November–January
HARVEST	October

Cover your ears and eyes those of a delicate disposition, but you can't talk about medlars without saying (quietly perhaps) 'dog's arse'. Looking much like small, flattened russet apples, medlars have an open end away from the stem that looks unmistakably like a canine's behind. The similarity wasn't lost on the Victorians who christened them somewhat frankly, as did the French and many others, so you can blame them, not me, for any offence taken.

Thankfully the flavour is altogether more appealing – somewhere between an apple and a date. Its truly unique deep, musky and winey taste sits happily next to and within sweet and savoury dishes. The classic recipes of medlar jelly and medlar cheese, sweet as they may be, belong more to the savoury shelf with their affinity with almost any meat and cheese.

Medlars also make beautifully untamed trees, throwing out randomly twisting arms. They really aren't candidates for being trained and constrained to fit wires or flattened against a wall, but let them do their own thing and you'll be rewarded with one of the more characterful small trees you can have in your garden. It will give you rich autumn colours with its leaves, and once they've fallen the delectable fruit will be left hanging like Christmas decorations – perfect for picking after the first frosts.

Varieties

I've never had a bad medlar – every variety seems to be equally tasty. They are self-fertile too. 'Nottingham' is probably the most widely available and has grown and fruited happily for me. It's worth looking out for 'Royal' too – its larger fruit is a little quicker to deal with in the kitchen.

Growing

Growing food doesn't get much easier than a medlar. Plant it as outlined on p.146 and after any formative pruning to give a clear stem for a metre or so, allow it to ramble as it pleases. You may want to just control its spread if it tries to get too large for your site with a little careful pruning in winter.

The wild rose-like flowers appear on the tips of sideshoots and spurs, developing into the characteristic fruits. Take a few moments to enjoy them in spring – they're like lazy dog rose flowers.

Pull any suckers (shoots appearing from the base) as soon as you spot them: cutting can leave short stubs to regrow while pulling is more likely to remove any dormant buds that may throw out suckers the following year.

Harvesting and storage

Medlars are usually enjoyed after they've started to soften and bruise (known as bletting). To get them in this state you can either pick them in mid-autumn when they are still hard and allow them to blet indoors, or wait a few weeks until the frost hits them and race the wildlife to pick the soft fallen ones. You can also hasten the bletting process by giving firm medlars a night in the freezer. I usually pick some medlars early to blet a little indoors, as this is perfect for making jelly, whereas fully soft fruit is ideal for any other use.

Try to pick them on a dry day, to keep moisture on the fruit to a minimum.

Pests and diseases

Medlars are pretty untroubled by ailments, although hawthorn leaf spot can be a problem. It shows as multiple brown leaf spots, about 2mm in diameter, and there is no remedy other than collecting up and incinerating the leaves.

Eating

Medlars aren't for savouring fresh from the tree, they need cooking. Medlar jelly and jam are as fine as any. They also work well in mincemeat – especially paired with that other forgotten fruit, quince. I made a medlar version of the chestnut jam in Pam Corbin's *Preserves* handbook: runnier than most jams, it's more of a sauce and perfect with pancakes or drop scones.

Bake or quarter and gently stew a few handfuls of medlars, then sieve and sweeten to taste and you'll have a rich and datey purée that's a delicious change in creamy recipes such as the mess (p.224) and cranachan (p.218).

Recipes Medlar jelly (p.220).

Fallen medlars ready for picking

Melon 'Minnesota Midget'

Melons *Cucumis melo*

SOW	March–April
HARVEST	August–October

One of the few annual fruits, melons bring a welcome couple of weeks of the exotic to the garden. They look and taste like the slightly wayward children that a cucumber and a squash might come up with, although much, much sweeter and far more succulent than either.

Melons are reliant on getting the heat and sunshine they crave to ripen their fruit, but with the right varieties, a little care and a half-decent summer, the gamble is one worth taking. Growing them under cover, with a little help from a cloche, and/or near a sunny wall, will edge the odds strongly in your favour.

With luck you'll have melons that are far more luscious and aromatic than the ones you're used to buying because you can pick them at their just-ripe peak.

There are three main types of melon: honeydew, which usually have yellow flesh, a firm texture and keep well; musk, with skin that looks as if it's covered in netting, green or orange flesh and which are generally only fruitful under cover; and cantaloupe, usually with ribbed skin and orange flesh. Cantaloupe types need less heat and sun to ripen and are the best options for cooler parts of the country.

Varieties

Many new varieties are being developed which need fewer sunshine hours to ripen, and concentrate energies on fruit production rather than green growth. It's fair to say that these may be your most reliable route to ripe melons, but I think many of the older varieties have the edge on flavour.

'Blenheim Orange' is my favourite of the musk melons, 'Sweetheart' is a fine cantaloupe that's reliable indoors or out, and 'Rocky Ford Honey Dew' is as good as I've had of the honeydews.

Watermelons, although loosely considered as melons, belong to a different family (*Citrullus lanatus*). 'Sugar Baby' is delicious, but needs a lot of water and sunshine to ripen.

Growing

Melons are annuals – sown, grown and harvested within the year. Start them off in small pots in late March or early April on your windowsill, with up to four well-spaced seeds per pot. They tend to germinate well and grow strongly. Water them so that they're moist (but not wet) most of the time. Any extra warmth (from a heated propagator or on a windowsill near a radiator) will move things along well. When the roots have developed and three or four leaves have grown, pot them on into 10–12cm pots.

If you are growing melons outside, harden your plants off, by leaving them outside during the day, and bringing them back indoors at night, for about 2 weeks in early May. This will acclimatise them to outdoor conditions and temperature swings. From late May, plant them outside in a sunny, sheltered patch, under a cloche if you have one for speedier growth, or against a south-facing wall.

If you're growing melons under cover you can plant them without hardening off in mid-May.

Melons like a well-drained, humus-rich soil to grow in. Ensure the soil is loose at the bottom of the hole, so that the roots have an easy route down and out in search of much-needed water and nutrients.

Plant your seedlings just below the top of the root system – don't overdo this as planting too deep can lead to rotting. You can plant them on a small mound of soil, watering sparingly into a moat around the mound until the plant gets to a good size.

Allow 50cm or so distance from their neighbour if growing them up a cane, or twice that if allowing them to scramble willy-nilly.

Water the plants only a little at first to minimise the risk of rotting, increasing gradually as the plant grows. A comfrey feed (or similar, see p.161) every week or so from when flowering starts will really help productivity. Water and feed little and often (rather than deluge at lengthy intervals) as the fruit swells.

Melons are self-fertile, producing both male and female flowers on each plant. They're easy to tell apart – the female flowers have a round swelling at the base of the petals where the fruit will develop. When flowers appear, use a small, soft, dry paintbrush to lightly brush pollen from male flowers onto female flowers to promote good pollination. The best time to do this is in the middle of a hot, humid day.

Netting comes in useful with melons. They are vines that will naturally clamber up or scramble across netting, and keeping the plant largely off the ground helps to reduce the likelihood of disease and rotting.

Don't be tempted to pinch out sideshoots, as this is where flowers develop, but do snip off the growing tips a couple of leaves beyond any fruit. This diverts energies towards the fruit rather than unnecessary green growth.

Having run the gauntlet of researching melons at length on the internet, I've discovered that – rather fittingly – the support the fruit require once they reach tennis-ball size can be most ably provided by an old brassiere. Lacy is best, allowing more light and air through for even ripening. Tights will do equally, if not quite as poetically, well.

Harvesting and storage

Melons enjoy a long season of sun and most will be ready at the end of summer, perhaps even the start of autumn, depending on the variety and how the summer has been. The scent is the giveaway: it should be deep, rich and musky. The skin around the stalk may also start to split and soften, while the south pole of the melon (i.e. away from the stalk) should give a little to thumb pressure. Cut, rather than pull, the fruit from the plant.

Melons will be OK in the fridge for a few days, but do let them get to room temperature for a couple of hours before eating – they'll be better than those you can buy but they never quite recapture that just-picked loveliness.

Pests and diseases

Melons need water, but too much early on can lead to neck rot, where the roots rot away, killing the plant.

Powdery mildew can be a problem, so remove and burn any affected leaves as soon as they're spotted. Red spider mite (see p.179) and whitefly can be problematic to melons grown indoors. Whitefly suck the sap of many plants, encouraging moulds and weakening the plant. It thrives in hot conditions and is usually only a problem for plants grown under cover. Treat with biological control (see Directory, pp. 248–9 for suppliers). Slugs and snails are their usual tedious selves – take whichever measures you favour (see p.180).

Cucumber mosaic virus appears as a mosaic pattern on the leaves and in stunted growth. There is no cure, so burn infected plants immediately and wash your hands and any tools that have come into contact with affected plants to avoid passing it on.

To avoid diseases building up in the soil, don't grow melons in the same bed 2 years in a row.

Eating

One of the loveliest cool garden treats, melons are best treated simply. Their refreshing, grassy sweetness makes for wonderful chilled soups, sorbets and salads, especially in combination with a little mint. For a simple but delicious soup to serve 6, peel, deseed and cube 2 perfectly ripe melons and zap them in a blender with 3 tbsp honey and the juice of 2 lemons. Serve well chilled with a few finely chopped mint and/or basil leaves scattered over.

Recipes Fruity melons (p.223) and Melon salad with goat's cheese, mint and red onion (p.222).

Mulberry 'King James'

Mulberries *Morus* spp.

PRUNE	March–April
HARVEST	August–September

My favourite fruit of all. The first time I ate them was only ten or so years ago. Friends had an ancient tree in their garden and I happened to be staying at just the right time. I wasn't expecting anything too good – I still assumed that if something was tasty it would be widely available – but they were incredible. If you've yet to try them (they're rarely in the shops), look forward to a deeper, winier version of a raspberry with an edge of blackcurrant to it, and a gentle sherbertiness. Comparing their delightful flavour with that of other fruit (and confectionery) doesn't do them full justice – they are utterly delicious.

You won't need to worry about any frosts damaging your chances of fruit: mulberry leaves and flowers are shy of the cold and burst late, providing a reliable signal that spring is properly upon us and the frosts behind. Even with this late kick-off they get their fruit grown and ripened quickly, usually by late July/early August, which makes them a great choice for anyone in a colder area where some of the more frost-susceptible fruit is particularly marginal.

Like medlars, mulberries are beautifully individual in their growth, throwing entirely random shapes that defy any sense of order you might have for them. They're lazily charming, which along with their large pointing-heart leaves, makes mulberries almost as rewarding for their looks as their fruit.

Varieties

Mulberries come in black, white and red varieties – don't let this concern you too much as their fruit doesn't necessarily correlate in colour, so a red mulberry may have black fruit. It is choice of variety that is all-important with mulberries. Many are delicious but most take time to start fruiting – often over 10 years. 'Illinois Everbearing', 'Carman', and 'Ivory' are a few of those that will get started after 3 years or so – and once you've tasted mulberries you won't want to wait too long for your own. Mulberries are self-fertile, so growing a single tree is fine.

Growing

Mulberries are easy to grow, needing almost no pruning and attracting few pests or diseases. Plant them as you would most trees (see p.146), in a sunny, sheltered position, avoiding chalky sites. Water in dry periods, especially when the tree is carrying fruit. Prune out any parts that die back after the winter cold.

Inside the canopy of a mulberry

Harvesting and storage

Mulberries ripen their fruit on older wood, during late summer, when the berries become sweet, soft and juicy. They are delicate, so while they can stain clothes, hand-picking is much better than anything too rough.

Perfectly ripe mulberries keep for a very short window (at least part of the reason why you'll very rarely see them for sale), so eat them quickly after harvesting, preferably as they are or treated simply.

Pests and diseases

Slugs love mulberry leaves and can cause serious damage, even killing a young tree, so do use slug pubs, organic pellets and/or go on slug hunts at dusk.

Eating

Please don't mess about with mulberries. Eat as many as you can as you pick them. Any left are fabulous in place of other berries in any of the recipes and the warming qualities of mulberry vodka are so great that it's worth having a cold winter to fully appreciate them. Follow the process for Quince vodka (see p.233) using 500g mulberries, 700ml vodka (or gin) and 160g sugar.

Recipes Mulberry mess (p.224). See also variations for crumble (p.239), clafoutis (p.209), tart (p.214), granita (p.243), trifle (p.244) and cranachan (p.218).

Peach 'Peregrine'

Peaches and nectarines
Prunus persica

PRUNE	May–June
HARVEST	July–September

I can think of no other homegrown food that is so unlike that which you buy in the shops than a peach or a nectarine. Warm from the tree, the fruit is an experience, rather than simply a revelation of flavour.

You'll need patience and considerable restraint to stop yourself picking the tempting fruit when it reaches visual perfection, so possibly handcuff yourself for a few days until your nose fills with the scent of intense peach. The fruit should almost fall into your hand at this point, with only the light touch of your fingers for encouragement.

Peaches and nectarines are far from certs to produce every year – you will need a sunny, well-drained, sheltered site, no late frosts, a reasonable summer and a willingness to employ a wrapping of nocturnal horticultural fleece around the flowers if the temperatures plummet. But if you can sidestep the late frosts, a peach or nectarine tree will reward you well.

And the difference between the two: a single gene which makes peaches gently furry and nectarines smooth.

Varieties

'Peregrine' has a reputation for being the most flavoursome variety, but I find 'Red Haven' and 'Rochester' equally delicious, while much more resistant to leaf curl. Don't believe the hype about 'Avalon Pride' being immune to leaf curl. Not only is it far from the finest-flavoured variety, the 40 trees I have grown at River Cottage and Otter Farm became riddled with leaf curl. As for nectarines, 'Pineapple' and the slightly more leaf-curl resistant 'Flavourtop' are the two choicest nectarines in my view.

Most peaches and nectarines are grafted onto 'St Julien A' rootstock (semi-vigorous, 5–6m height).

'Nectarella' nectarine and 'Bonanza' peach are dwarf varieties that grow slowly to only 1.3m or so, needing no pruning at all, and are the perfect choice for growing in a pot (minimum 50cm diameter).

Both peaches and nectarines are self-fertile, so you can grow a single tree, should you so wish.

Growing

Choose your site well, giving your tree shelter and sunshine. Plant as you would any fruit tree (see p.146), ensuring a good well-drained, fertile soil. Flowering time is the crucial period when you'll need to pay attention. Growing later-flowering varieties helps avoid the potential for frost damage, which would ruin any prospect of fruiting. But if you want to up your chances even more, get ready with some horticultural fleece to protect the blossom from cold night-time temperatures, making sure you get it off early in the morning so that pollination can take place. Hand pollinating (see p.189) with a soft, dry brush, every day through flowering if you can, will really increase the likelihood of fruit – especially in years where the blossom comes early and there are few pollinating insects around.

From the emergence of blossom, give the tree a good feed with comfrey liquid every fortnight to promote good fruit development.

Spacing depends on your chosen rootstock, but 6m is usual for larger trees. You can thin the growing fruit when they are small, or if any are wedged between branches or against a wall, so that the remaining fruit are 10cm or so apart. Those left on the tree should grow on more reliably to full-sized fruit.

Nectarines and peaches both take well to fan training (see pp.156–8), as well as being grown freestanding as a bush or pyramid.

The initial training of freestanding peaches and nectarines is as for plums (see p.154); you're after an open-centred bush or well-balanced pyramid. Once established, prune every summer and when doing so think of the next growing season. Peaches and nectarines fruit on branches and shoots grown the previous year so you'll want to snip out older wood to allow newer growth to develop and fruit. Cut back to a growth bud (these are pointed, while the fruit buds are fatter), to encourage new shoots which may bear fruit the next year. Remove any dead, diseased or damaged branches.

As with all stone fruit trees, pruning should take place on a dry, sunny day in late spring or summer to minimise the likelihood of silver leaf (see p.180) and bacterial canker (see p.176). Disinfect your secateurs after pruning each tree to avoid disease contamination.

Harvesting and storage

Depending on the variety, where you are in the country and the nature of the summer, your fruit should be ready from late July through August. Ripening occurs gradually over the tree, so you'll need to harvest daily once they get going.

Allow the fruit to develop its distinctive deep aroma – this can be a few days after you think it looks ready to eat, but be patient. Cup your hand around the fruit very gently (as if the peach was a cracked egg) and give a slow half-twist without any downward pull. When it's perfectly ready, the fruit will surrender.

Pests and diseases

While you can grow peaches and nectarines out in the open, if you train them against a sunny wall or grow dwarf varieties in pots it is much easier to protect them from their main enemy, leaf curl (see p.178), by covering or taking potted dwarf varieties indoors.

If you are growing your peaches and nectarines under cover, red spider mite (see p.179) can trouble them, as can brown scale (see p.177).

Eating

So fine are homegrown peaches and nectarines that it's almost inconceivable that you'll not eat them all fresh, beneath the tree. If the summer fades before all your peaches and nectarines are perfectly ripe then a gentle poaching in white wine with a few aromatic spices such as star anise, cloves and cinnamon is all they need to draw out the flavour and soften them beautifully.

Nectarines and peaches both have an affinity with cream, milk and yoghurt, so try them in smoothies too.

Recipes Peach (or nectarine) salsa (p.227) and Fruity melons (p.223). See also variations for apricots on toast (p.199), cranachan (p.218), fool (p.213) cake (p.232) and pear and rocket salad (p.228).

Immature nectarine fruit

Pears *Pyrus communis*

PRUNE	November–February
HARVEST	August–November

Pears, as Eddie Izzard noted, are 'gorgeous little beasts, but they're ripe for half an hour, and you're never there'. An exaggeration perhaps, but one that's not too far from the truth.

Pears are less of an instant pleasure than apples, most of which you can munch straight off the tree, but they are worth the gentle inconvenience. You pick them early and firm to ripen indoors, and while this delays the eating, it does mean few are troubled by pests or damaged while harvesting.

Pear trees can take a while to start fruiting properly and they don't take kindly to the cold or an imperfect supply of water. However, if you choose the most suitable varieties and eat them right at the ripe point, then you can expect a depth and complexity of flavour, as well as a succulence, that's of a different order entirely from those in the shops.

Varieties

'Conference' and 'Doyenne du Comice' are commonly grown in the UK and both are reliable and relatively easy to coax a good harvest out of. These varieties ripen in October–November.

Of the many other varieties, my favourites are: 'Beurre Giffard', which gives melting, winey early pears that are ready to eat in August; 'Fondante d'Automne' with its musky, lightly russeted fruit in September–October; 'Louise Bonne of Jersey' with its aromatic pears ready in October; and the late 'Glou Morceau', ready in time to see the New Year in.

A few new varieties are self-fertile and if you have room for only one pear then do make sure you choose one of these. That said, self-fertile varieties will crop better with a pollinating partner nearby. As with apples, the pollination group of your chosen varieties should be the same or from an adjacent group. Occasionally neighbours remain stubbornly incompatible (I know how they feel); for example 'Doyenne du Comice' and 'Onward' should, but won't pollinate each other. Check with your nursery.

Pears are usually grafted onto 'Quince A' (semi-vigorous, 4–6m height) or 'Quince C' (semi-dwarfing, 2.5–5m height) rootstocks.

A family tree (see p.24), where more than one variety is grafted onto a single stem, is also an option.

Pear 'Concorde'

Growing

Pears can be a little temperamental but so many of the best varieties aren't available in the shops that it makes the little effort required more than worthwhile. All but 'Conference', which can rough it a little, require a sheltered, sunny location with a fertile, well-drained soil, ideally neutral or slightly acidic. Avoid sandy soils.

Plant your tree as suggested on p.146, spaced 5m from its neighbour if on 'Quince A' rootstock, or 3.5m if on 'Quince C'.

Pears take well to espalier training (plant at least 2.5m apart), as well as single and double cordons (80cm and 1.5m apart respectively), and stepovers (see p.128).

Pear trees are pruned and trained as for apples (see p.153), and almost all are spur-bearers.

Water pear trees through any extended dry periods in summer and add well-rotted manure as a fertilising top dressing around (but not touching) the base in early spring. A good feed with compost or well-rotted manure every late winter or early spring can make all the difference to your harvest.

Harvesting and storage

There are three stages to bear in mind when harvesting pears: picking, storing and ripening.

You'll almost always pick pears while they're hard. They need time in a cool, dry, dark place (a garage is ideal) to mature. Judging the time for picking is the key. Firstly, ask your supplier (or look online) for the approximate time of picking for your variety, and then you'll need to be eagle-eyed for one or more of the following: the first windfalls; an often subtle lightening or flushing of the skin; and if, when you cup a pear and lift it upwards and gently twist, it separates from the tree with the stalk intact. It sounds like it might be a fuss but if you relax and check frequently one or more of those signs will show itself.

You can also try the taste test: the pears will be hard to the bite but when ready they should be sweet. This works for all except late-season pears, which are best cup-lift-twist tested.

Don't be tempted to leave pears too long on the tree. Left past the right point they can go 'sleepy' (grainy, soft and sometimes brown) in storage.

Store them in a single layer, not touching each other. Don't be tempted to bring them straight into the house to ripen – they usually either refuse to soften or go mealy. Regularly check pears while they're in storage and remove any showing signs of rot. Bring them into the main part of the house a few days before you want to eat them to allow them to ripen nicely.

Check ripening pears regularly. If you don't keep half an eye on them they'll take the opportunity to turn from stone to mush while you're out of the room making a cup of tea.

Pests and diseases

Pears can suffer from scab (see p.180) and fireblight (see p.178). Pear leaf blister mite causes blistering, and pear midges can cause leaves to roll up; in both cases, pull off and burn any affected leaves.

Eating

Wonderful in leafy or fruit salads, pears work exceptionally well with salty foods – blue and goat's cheeses and air-dried ham especially – as well as walnuts, pecans and hazelnuts.

If you're impatient, have a glut or are just looking for another way to treat pears, you can eat them early, poaching them to soften in white wine or sugar syrup with aromatic flavourings, such as bay, cloves, star anise, cinnamon and/or a vanilla pod.

Recipes Poached pears and chocolate sauce (p.231), Orchard ice cream with caramelised walnuts (p.195), Fruity melons (p.223) and Pear and rocket salad with Blue Vinny and walnuts (p.228). See also variations for melon salad (p.222), compote (p.200), clafoutis (p.209), cake (p.232) and vodka (p.233).

Pear 'Louise Bonne of Jersey' in storage

Plum 'Purple Pershore'

Plums, damsons, bullaces and gages *Prunus domestica* and *Prunus insititia*

PRUNE	May–June
HARVEST	July–October

Last summer I picked the first basket of Dittisham plums, eating a fair few while I was at it and on the walk back to the house. The rest went into a bowl. Within a couple of hours the house was filled with a heavy, sweet, invisible cloud of plum. A more perfect alternative to those hideous plug-in room fresheners I can't imagine.

The recipe for this house-filling perfume is a simple one. Find a fruit nursery that specialises in local varieties and tell them about your proposed site; buy two varieties for best pollination (and therefore fruiting); then wait a couple of years at most. Every summer thereafter you'll be able to enjoy the aroma – and the taste.

There is a rather fuzzy line between plums, damsons, bullaces and greengages. All plums and gages are varieties of *Prunus domestica*, with gages (sweet, green plums brought to the UK from France 300 years ago) tending to be sweeter and more spherical than plums. Damsons and bullaces are varieties of *Prunus insititia*, producing smaller fruits than their relatives, on small, hardy trees. Both fruits tend to be flavoursome but tart, excellent for cooking rather than eating fresh. You'll find damsons, bullaces and gages much less frequently in the shops, so do consider them for a space in your garden.

The markings on plum stones are unique to each variety, a fruity fingerprint of sorts. When Henry VIII's flagship, the *Mary Rose*, was raised after 450 years at the bottom of the sea, over 100 varieties of plum stone were found – a clue to the importance of plums in our diet at the time, and our appreciation of the range of flavours and textures plums and their relatives offer. You'll be lucky to find 50 tree varieties available now.

Varieties

Grow two if you can – even self-fertile varieties fruit more reliably with a compatible partner. Or if growing one tree, make it a self-fertile variety and use a soft brush to move pollen from one blossom to another. You can choose plums that will fruit in early, mid or late season but as with apples, you'll need to ensure your varieties belong to coinciding or adjacent pollination groups.

'Victoria' is a reliable, high-yielding, self-fertile cooker/eater and an excellent choice for a single tree, but there are finer-flavoured plums out there if you have room for two or more trees. 'Jefferson', 'Rivers' Early Prolific', 'Pershore Yellow Egg' and 'Kirke's Blue' are fabulous, but do look into your local and other vanishing varieties. There are some spectacularly tasty gems out there.

If you're after a later-ripening variety, 'Marjorie's Seedling' will give you plums as late as October some years.

'Blue Violet' (from the Lake District), 'Farleigh Damson' and 'Dittisham Damson' are my favourite of the damsons.

All the bullace varieties I've tried have been equally delicious, less fine for eating fresh but all good for making excellent preserves.

Do try gages. 'Oullin's Gage' (self-fertile) is great for cooking or eating fresh and its tendency to flower late gives the blossom a better chance of missing any late frosts. 'Coe's Golden Drop' and 'Golden Transparent' are wonderfully sweet too.

As with pears, some from the same or adjacent pollination groups refuse to pollinate each other: 'Rivers' Early Prolific' and 'Jefferson'; 'Cambridge Gage' and 'Old Green Gage', for example. Check with your supplier for incompatibilities.

Mirabelles, also known as cherry plums, are popularly grown in France but comparatively rare here, yet their apricot-sized fruit is delicious, ripening more quickly than plums. Mirabelles are also hardier than many plums, making them a great choice for growing in the UK. 'Golden Sphere' and 'Gypsy' are both good.

Most plums and their close relatives are grafted onto 'St Julien A' (semi-vigorous, 2.5–3m height) or 'Pixy' (semi-dwarfing, 2–2.2m height).

Growing

Plums and their near relatives enjoy a fertile, well-drained soil in a sunny, sheltered position. They are a little particular when it comes to water, as they like a reasonable amount of it through the warmer months but hate waterlogged soils at any time of the year. A heavyish but well-drained site is ideal. If your position doesn't quite match up to this, you can add plenty of organic matter to help retain water. Make sure you water the tree in the first year and through any extended dry spells. Mulching generously every spring particularly helps to retain precious water.

The trees themselves are generally very hardy but flowering is the crunch time. They usually blossom early and can be very susceptible to frosts killing off the flowers – and your chances of fruit. Avoid frost pockets or windy sites and (if you can be bothered) use horticultural fleece on cold nights once the flowers appear, removing it early in the morning so pollination isn't compromised.

Flowers are carried mainly at the base of year-old shoots and along the length of 2-year-old shoots, as well as any fruiting spurs.

Fruit is usually thinned as it develops, especially in the early years. This involves snipping out some when they're small and still green, leaving around 8cm between fruit. Those remaining will develop much more happily. Thinning also helps those varieties (such as 'Victoria') that are prone to one heavy harvest followed by a much lesser one to have a more consistent harvest. Branches are less likely to snap under the weight of developing fruit too. Don't be alarmed if the tree sheds some fruit; known as 'June drop', this is just its way of managing the crop it can handle.

Plums and their close relations are happily grown as bushes or pyramids, or trained as cordons, minarettes or fans (see p.128). It's easier if you buy them part trained. Once the initial pruning is done, keep pruning to an absolute minimum, as it invites diseases. Just take out dead, diseased, damaged or crossing branches from freestanding trees in summer and prune fans as described on pp.156–8.

With a dwarfing rootstock such as 'Pixy', plums can be grown in large pots but watering is critical as any drying out can stress the plant and reduce productivity.

Harvesting and storage

Depending on the variety, location and the type of summer, plums, damsons and gages can be ready to harvest between July and mid-October.

The first few fruits dropping of their own accord is the green light for picking. Colour is a reasonable indicator of readiness but not as accurate as aroma and the ease of separating the fruit from the tree. The fruit ripens gradually across the tree so you'll need to harvest in more than one visit. Pick carefully to avoid bruising the delicate fruit and, if possible, leave a short stalk to keep the fruit and next year's buds intact. The fruit should give up their grip with the gentlest of persuasion.

Pests and diseases

Silver leaf disease (see p.180) is the most likely nuisance and minimising pruning helps enormously in reducing the likelihood. Brown rot (see p.177), blossom wilt (see p.176), bacterial canker (see p.176) and rust (see p.179) can occur. Gummy spots of resin appearing on the bark is usually a sign of stress.

Aphids may appear in early spring but rarely do more than cosmetic damage, though it can be worth stringing up pheromone traps in mid-May to trap male plum moths and prevent their larvae decimating your ripening fruit.

Eating

Plums and their relations are among the most rewarding of fruits to grow. Available in sweet or sharper varieties, they offer endless culinary possibilities. Eaten fresh as they're picked, stewed into a compote to enjoy hot or cold, baked in a clafoutis, cake, crumble or tart, or even left in a jar with sugar and vodka, they are superb.

Recipes Plum and hazelnut cake (p.232). See also variations for apricots on toast (p.199), baked figs (p.211), compote (p.200), clafoutis (p.209), crumble (p.239), tart (p.214), cranachan (p.218), fool (p.213), granita (p.243) and vodka (p.233).

Quince 'Meeches Prolific'

Quince *Cydonia oblonga*

PRUNE	November–February
HARVEST	October

Quince are about deferred culinary pleasure. There is no luscious, succulent, aromatic loveliness to pick from the tree; you have to wait a little longer. You'll almost always pick quince hard, sharp and by all immediate culinary measures inedible. But once indoors quince will ripen gradually, and as the fruit sweetens and softens it releases a perfume that lifts the entire house.

Quince are now fairly uncommon in this country, but it wasn't always this way. King Edward I planted the first quince on these shores in the grounds of the Tower of London 800 years ago. They gained and retained popularity for all but the last century when we became keener on increasingly available and more 'immediate' exotic fruit. They are enjoying something of a resurgence, but you'll still rarely find quince for sale, so you may have to grow a tree to enjoy this marvellous fruit.

Varieties

'Meeches Prolific' and 'Vranja' both ripen early and are reliably heavy croppers, bearing large, delicious fruit. They fruit early in life and although all quince are self-fertile they will pollinate each other, meaning you get a larger crop. 'Leskovac' and 'Krymsk' are newer, similarly delicious varieties that show promise of ripening fully on the tree in good, long sunny summers.

Quince are one of the few trees usually grown on its own rootstock: 'Quince A' for a plant 4–4.5m high; 'Quince C' for one 3–3.5m.

Growing

Quince like the same conditions as most fruit trees: shelter, good sunshine and a good fertile soil. They will be happy in a moist (but not waterlogged) soil but don't try growing them in alkaline conditions as they like neutral to mildly acidic soils. Plant as outlined on p.146, allowing 5m or so from its neighbour, or 4m if you've chosen a tree on a 'Quince C' rootstock. Quince are low-maintenance trees, requiring only watering through dry periods. A good spring mulch is worth the trouble, keeping the roots cool and retaining precious water.

Flowers develop mainly at the end of year-old stems, with some also on short spurs. The fruit follows quickly but can be a little discouraging – sitting there, mostly unchanging for a few summer months until autumn approaches, when the small nuggets become plump.

Quince flowering

Give your quince a monthly comfrey tea or seaweed feed (see p.161), by leaf spraying or watering around the roots, from the start of flowering through to harvesting, and you're likely to have a larger crop.

Prune quince trees in winter to establish a goblet shape, but do remember that they are naturally erratic in shape and will throw random twists and arcs. Don't be too strict with them if you want to release their full charm. And bearing in mind they are predominantly tip-bearing, don't remove much in the way of year-old stems. Once established, prune out dead, diseased or congested growth only.

Harvesting and storage

Quince are usually picked unripe in early autumn, when they separate from the tree easily without twisting or yanking. Hard and sour before fully ripened, quince will ripen in storage or in a bowl in the house. You'll know when they've got there as you'll have a house full of their incredible scent. Don't pick them too soon – every extra day will be of benefit to the fruit – but do make sure you get them in before the first frosts.

You'll have plenty of time to enjoy your quince as they usually store well into (and occasionally through) winter. Keep quince separate from other fruits in storage – their perfume may taint them.

Pests and diseases

Quince are susceptible to powdery mildews (see p.179), brown rot (see p.177) and fireblight (see p.178). Quince leaf blight can be a nuisance too, showing itself as small brown dots on the leaves, which, although usually cosmetic only, can develop into serious infections that stress the tree considerably. Rake up any affected fallen leaves and burn them to reduce the likelihood of repetition the following year. If your tree has had a bad infection, consider spraying with Bordeaux mixture (a copper-based fungicide) as the leaves emerge the following spring.

Eating

As with pears, quince are rarely ready to eat straight from the tree. Once they reach their aromatic peak they are ready to core, stuff with butter and sugar and bake – to be eaten warm with yoghurt or ice cream, added sparingly to apple pies and tarts to give a hint of their lovely perfume and colour, or to be made into membrillo (quince cheese), a firm jelly that's incredible, especially with cheese.

Recipes Orchard ice cream with caramelised walnuts (p.195) and Quince vodka (p.233). See also variations for pear and rocket salad (p.228), tagine (p.196), poached pears (p.231), compote (p.200), crumble (p.239), granita (p.243), jelly (p.220) and fruit leather (p.234).

Raspberries *Rubus idaeus*

PRUNE	September–November, February–March
HARVEST	July–November

Everybody should grow raspberries, they are so easy and delicious. It should be the law. All that lovely sweet-sharpness for virtually no effort.

Greek myth has it that all raspberries were once white, until the nymph Ida, while picking wild raspberries for Jupiter, pricked her finger on the thorns, her blood staining the fruit from that moment on. You may struggle to find white raspberries, but yellow varieties are sold widely and tend to dodge the birds' attention more than red ones.

I'm not a great one for getting too deeply into the botanicals, but occasionally it's worthwhile, especially when it shines a light on something in the kitchen. Raspberries are a case in point. They aren't berries as such, but clusters of drupelets. Each of these individual bobbles of the 'berry' is a fruit in itself, enclosing its own seed, and attached to its neighbours by the fine threads that look like micro-hairs. This binding allows the cluster of drupelets to stay together, coming away from the core intact when picked. It gives them their characteristic hollow centre, which rather pleasingly scoops up cream.

Varieties

Raspberries are self-fertile and come in summer-fruiting and autumn-fruiting varieties that can be equally delicious, although they behave a little differently from each other and have a few differing requirements, as detailed below. If you have the space it's good to grow both to enjoy a long, tasty season. Of the summer varieties, I like 'Glen Moy' (spineless too), 'Glen Ample' and 'Glen Magna'. 'Autumn Bliss' and the yellow 'Allgold' are my favourite autumn-fruiters.

Growing

Raspberries are fairly tolerant of most situations, apart from alkaline soils. Neutral to slightly acidic soils, rich in organic matter, are ideal. Any mulching you can give your plants will help to retain the moisture raspberries need. Shelter and sun are vital for the largest crop.

Plant raspberries 45cm or so apart, with 2m between rows for summer varieties and 1m for autumn cultivars. Don't plant them with their roots spread wide, or too deeply as raspberries are shallow-rooting. Some people snip off the top of the cane after planting, to just above a bud, 25cm above ground level.

Raspberry 'Glen Ample'

Trained raspberries

Summer raspberries, harvested in the hottest months, produce fruit on canes that grew the year before, so you'll not get fruit in the first summer. Each cane fruits only once, so remove fruited canes after harvesting, leaving room for new canes to grow through. Tie canes to horizontal wires as they grow to stop them flailing around and the older shoots from snapping in the wind.

Autumn raspberries ripen their fruit on the current year's canes so after you've enjoyed the fruit from them they won't produce any more the next year. Wait until late winter then cut all the canes to the ground. As new shoots grow steadily in early summer thin them to avoid overcrowding, leaving 8cm or so between developing canes. You can support the growing shoots by tying them to horizontal wires. Alternatively, be lazy and just snip out overcrowded patches and let your raspberries grow as a hedge – they'll look less classically beautiful but be very productive.

Raspberries can spread sideways by growing suckers. If an expanding raspberry patch isn't something you want, do pull them up as they appear.

After 10 years or so, raspberry plants decline in productivity and often become more susceptible to diseases, so after 8 or 9 years it pays to replace them with new canes. You can take advantage of their suckering habit as a cheap way of replenishing your stocks (see p.135). Plant them in a different part of your plot to minimise the likelihood of diseases building up.

Raspberries will do reasonably well in containers, if a little lower in yield, and you'll need to water and feed them regularly. Autumn varieties, being smaller, suit container growing best. Three canes in a 30cm diameter pot is about right. Be prepared to support them as they grow if necessary.

Harvesting and storage

Summer-fruiting varieties are usually ready from mid-June to mid-August, while autumn raspberries ripen from August to October.

Raspberries are perfectly ripe when a gentle pull separates the fruit from the plant, leaving the plug clean and intact – usually a day or two after they look ready. Any that you may have let go beyond perfect ripeness should still be picked and composted. This stimulates new fruit to develop, whereas any decaying fruit left on the plant will encourage pests and diseases.

Raspberries freeze well. To stop them clumping together, freeze in a single layer on a tray, then tip into a bag or tub when frozen – in quantities to suit.

Pests and diseases

Raspberries are susceptible to a number of viruses, which usually appear first as mottling and yellow blotching of the leaves or, in the case of cane blight and cane spot, as purple spots or black bases on the canes. Your plants will be weakened and your harvest limited. It pays to buy certified virus-free plants to keep your troubles to a minimum. There's no cure for most viruses, although some varieties are more resistant than others, and thinning encourages air circulation, which helps reduce the likelihood of infections. If your plants are affected, dig up and incinerate them immediately.

Birds can be a complete nuisance or they may ignore your raspberries entirely. Net your plants if the former.

Raspberry beetle will indicate its presence through dried patches at the stalk end of the fruit, usually around July, and you'll find a maggot. There is no cure, so if you see the adults, which are brown and 5mm long, squash them immediately. Autumn-fruiting varieties are less affected.

Eating

Raspberries will take happily to many of the recipes in this book, though you may prefer to enjoy them just as they are, or simply with cream or crème fraîche.

Recipes Raspberry fruit leather (p.234), Fruity melons (p.223), Bottled raspberries (p.236), Frozen summer berries and hot white chocolate sauce (p.201) and Summer pudding (p.202). See also variations for mess (p.224), fool (p.213), granita (p.243), trifle (p.244), cranachan (p.218), tart (p.214), crumble (p.239) and vodka (p.233).

Redcurrant 'Red Lake'

Redcurrants and white currants *Ribes rubrum*

PRUNE	May–June, November–January
HARVEST	July–August

Alongside medlars, red- and white currants make the finest jelly – especially good with lamb, game and cheese. Given that these soft fruits are rarely available in the shops and expensive when they are, this is reason alone to grow them.

Although red- and white currants are usually sharp and so best enjoyed in the kitchen, if you can be patient and have your currants netted against birds you may get to eat them deliciously sweet as you pick them. Not that sweeter is necessarily better, but by protecting your ripening currants you open up the possibility of a double harvest (as with gooseberries).

Usually 5–10mm in diameter, these currants hang in tassels, known as racemes or strigs, that poke through the leaves like a nosy neighbour. Both are keenly snaffled by birds, who are happy to nip them off one at a time as they mature, so do net them if you can, or if you can't, use bird-scarers of one kind or another (CDs swinging on string are great).

Varieties

'Jonkheer van Tets', 'Red Lake' and 'Redstart' are excellent redcurrant varieties, that ripen one after the other. Of the white currant varieties, 'White Versailles' is a long-established favourite and hard to rival as a reliable, flavoursome choice. 'Rovada' is also good and ripens after 'White Versailles', giving you a longer season if you grow both.

Growing

Red- and white currants are self-fertile and like a sheltered, well-drained spot with a fertile soil. They are best positioned in sun for the sweetest fruit, but they will tolerate a little shade, making them good for training against a shady wall.

Plant them 1.3m apart or 60cm from each other if grown as double cordons (See p.128). Plant bare-root currants in late autumn ideally (but no later than the end of winter). If you've bought container-grown plants, they may be planted at any time. Mulch plants every spring and water through extended dry periods.

Red- and white currants fruit on buds that form at the base of last year's new shoots. Whether grown as open bushes, standards, cordons or fans, red- and white

Fan-trained white currant

currants should be pruned hard in winter to take out unproductive and crossing branches. Prune sublaterals back to one bud to encourage new spurs, which will develop flowers and fruit.

Cordons should also be pruned as summer arrives: cut new sublaterals back to five leaves. In winter, cut back the leader to just above one bud of last year's growth and prune all sublaterals to two buds to encourage new fruiting spurs.

Whichever form you grow your red- or white currants in, use canes and twine to tie the branches, as they will become heavy when in fruit. Netting against birds is crucial unless you're happy to share much of your crop.

Currants are shallow-rooting and therefore happy to be grown in containers (30cm minimum diameter is ideal).

Harvesting and storage

The fruit is ready mid to late summer. Redcurrants become a lively red, with white currants developing a richer, creamy ivory colour. But be patient with redcurrants – they need a little longer after reddening to develop sweetness. Pinch them from the plant as whole trusses, running a fork down the trusses to release the currants. They tend to spoil fairly quickly in the fridge but freeze well – spread out in a single layer on a tray and freeze, before bagging them up in quantities to suit you.

Pests and diseases

Redcurrant blister aphids cause red blisters on redcurrant leaves in summer, and yellow blistering to white and blackcurrants. Check the underside of leaves in late spring for yellow aphids and remove them – but don't reach for the chemicals as the effect is only cosmetic – you'll still be in for fruit. If you do want to do something about the impact, try pyrethrum – an organic treatment made from the white flowerheads of the pyrethrum plant. Also, in mid-June, cut back the sideshoots to a centimetre or two short of the first fruit to remove any blistered leaves and encourage good air circulation around the fruit.

If your plants are affected by sawfly larvae or coral spot (see p.178), cut any affected shoots back to good wood and burn the prunings.

Eating

Red- and white currants make a fabulous jelly to complement meat and cheese, but for the most part they are better in a supporting role, bringing their colour and sweet/sharp edge to any number of puds.

Recipes Frozen summer berries and hot white chocolate sauce (p.201) and Summer pudding (p.202). See also variations for jelly (p.220), tart (p.214), fool (p.213), cranachan (p.218) and bottled fruit (p.236).

Forced 'Timperley Early' rhubarb

Rhubarb *Rheum* x *hybridum*

HARVEST	March–July

I couldn't be without rhubarb. I love its sour sharpness but as with all the kitchen-garden essentials, timing is what turns something fabulous into a real must-have. Depending on the variety, you can be pulling stalks from mid-April through summer but if you've a forcing pot (or a large bucket) you can not only get yourself an early harvest, you'll get one of the great treats of the edible garden.

A few square miles of Yorkshire countryside has the perfect conditions for growing the very finest rhubarb. With the right level of rain, ideal soil and waste wool, ashes and soot from the local nineteenth-century industries, a flourishing community of forced-rhubarb producers sprang up. Competition for the earliest sales (and therefore the best prices) drove new methods for growing until the classic outdoor-indoor method was found.

The plants are grown in the field for 2 years to give them a good start, then brought indoors each winter after a period of cold induces dormancy. The sheds are warm to cause the plant to awaken but, with the light excluded, the plant uses its own reserves (glucose in its base) to feed the early growth of new stalks. This happens at such a rate that you can hear the creaks and cracks of expansion.

Without light the rhubarb grows a wonderful livid pink with yellow leaves, instantly distinguishable from maincrop rhubarb. It is also more succulent and sweeter than the unhurried version. Harvested by candlelight, as exposure to strong light halts this type of growth, the forced rhubarb ensures a steady crop until the outdoor harvest begins.

You can replicate these conditions by placing a rhubarb forcer or a large bucket over the crowns in late winter. If you can pile fresh manure around it all the better; it's not essential but the raised temperature will speed up the growth even more. Your reward will be stunning stalks a good 4 or 5 weeks ahead of the main harvest. You may not want to do this for all your plants though, as once the forced crop is over you should leave your plants to recover over the spring and summer, ready to produce the following year. After harvesting, remove the forcer or bucket.

Varieties

'Timperley Early', 'Raspberry Red' and 'Victoria' are as good as any varieties, with 'Victoria' fruiting a little later than the other two. 'Timperley Early' produces earlier than most varieties, but it does have a fairly high chilling requirement (i.e. it needs lots of winter cold) and so is particularly suited to colder areas.

Rhubarb forcers

Growing

Rhubarb is pretty simple to grow – it's the courgette of the fruit world. You can buy young crowns or divide established ones (see p.135) to multiply your stock. If you are buying young crowns, allow the plant to establish for a year in the ground before harvesting more than the odd stalk.

Give your plant a rich, well-manured position in full sun, water it through dry periods, and you'll be able to return every day or two to pull repeated harvests through its season. Allow at least 90cm between plants.

If flowers appear, cut them off, as they reduce the vigour of the leafy stalk growth which is the part you want to eat. In autumn, as the foliage withers, remove dead leaves and add well-rotted manure and a good mulch to give them the best start to the following growing season.

Harvesting and storage

Depending on the variety and the sunniness of the season, you can be harvesting rhubarb from March until the end of July, when you should stop picking to allow the plant to grow and store reserves for the following year. For the most flavoursome, tender stalks, choose stems with good colour, where the leaves have just unfolded fully. Don't cut the stems – there's a knack to harvesting: grasp the stem low on the plant, and give a sharp pull-and-twist to remove the stalk cleanly.

Chop off leaves and get them straight into the compost heap; they're poisonous to eat so there's no point bringing them into the kitchen.

Pests and diseases

Rhubarb is pretty immune from diseases. If you notice limp foliage, weak stems and new buds dying off during the growing season your plant may have a fungal disease, crown rot. There's no alternative to digging the plant up, incinerating and planting new crowns.

Eating

Stewed gently with a little sugar or sweet cicely, rhubarb makes a great sauce for oily fish or poultry.

Rhubarb is also fabulous roasted. Cut into short lengths, lay in an ovenproof dish and grate the zest of an orange and a 3–4cm piece of fresh ginger over it. Dust with sugar, cover loosely with foil and roast in the oven at 160°C/Gas mark 3 for about 40 minutes until tender.

Recipes Rhubarb crumble (p.239) and Rhubarb and strawberry tart (p.240). See also variations for fool (p.213), mess (p.224), cranachan (p.218), trifle (p.244), tart (p.214) and granita (p.243).

Strawberry 'Honeoye'

Strawberries *Fragaria* x *ananassa*

HARVEST	May–October

Until last summer I had always been a little sniffy about strawberries. I love them as any sane person should, but given a straight choice, I'd have taken raspberries every time. I'm not so sure now. Last summer I grew six varieties and gave them a little more attention than I have in the past and they were extraordinary. I was even out there with the tennis racket for any wasps that got a little crabby when I was picking. I don't mind sharing a bit, but there are limits.

The secret seems to be getting belting varieties and preparing the ground with well-rotted manure and/or keeping up with the liquid feed from flowering onwards. I was expecting pleasant enough strawberries but, as with many fruits, the telltale sign is in the scent. When they're on their way to full ripeness the aroma draws you in. The wasps are awake to the fragrance too, so do set up wasp traps – not much beats the old 'jam round the rim/water in the bottom of the jar' treatment.

I know they're synonymous with Wimbledon but plant a few varieties that ripen in succession and your promise of a cream tea will last way beyond... even until October with a good summer and the right selection.

Varieties

I've found my favourite varieties come from the newest and the oldest available. 'Honeoye' is a delicious early-season strawberry, seeing you all through June, handing over the baton to 'Cambridge Favourite', an oldie, that is perfect for late June (i.e. Wimbledon) and all of July, even a little longer some years. 'Mara des Bois' is a perpetual fruiter, which, while not exactly up there with the self-refilling pint, does offer a sweet, aromatic, steady harvest from the second half of August into autumn. But the winner for flavour may well be 'Royal Sovereign' – not as high yielding or as large as some new varieties, but wait until you taste it.

Do consider alpine strawberries too, especially the variety 'Mignonette'. Easy to sow from seed, these non-spreading strawberries grow as medium-sized domes – showered in fruit from May right through the summer. The berries are too small for all but the most patient to pick in huge amounts. Instead, throw a handful into muffins, eat them warm from the plant, or allow a few to dissolve in a glass of sparkling wine.

Strawberries are self-fertile so growing one variety is fine.

Look for certified virus-free plants from a good supplier and plant them out as soon as you can after they arrive.

Growing

The ideal time to plant young strawberry plants is in late summer/early autumn, as this allows the roots to establish easily in soil that still has a little warmth. Planting later in autumn or even in spring is fine but don't expect a sizeable crop in the first year. Do choose a spot in full sun, where you haven't grown any of the *Solanaceae* family (such as potatoes and tomatoes) or chrysanthemums. These are all susceptible to verticillium wilt (leaves turn brown and wilt), which can kill your strawberries.

Prepare the ground well (see p.142) and trim any long roots and brown leaves off your plants. Dig a trench or holes and spread the roots widely, ensuring that the crown is level with the surface of the soil. Backfill and water well and gently firm in. Water well over the coming weeks while your plants establish.

Allow 50cm between plants and 90cm between rows ideally, although you can squeeze this by a third if you have very fertile ground and/or are growing your strawberries in raised beds.

Strawberries are shallow-rooting and are likely to suffer in dry periods and from weed competition, so as the first fruits appear, lay straw between the plants and under the developing fruit to suppress weeds, retain water and prevent water splash on the berries, which can lead them to turn mouldy.

After you've harvested all the berries, snip off all old fruiting stems, runners and leaves, give your strawberry bed a good comfrey feed and add more well-rotted manure. This will give the plants a boost, encouraging them to throw out some new healthy growth, which will set them up for the following year's cropping.

Strawberry plants will produce well for 4 years or so, but after this you should replace them with new plants. By changing your plants in a staggered system (say around one third each year), you'll spread the expenditure and never leave yourself without fruit.

To create new plants, you can propagate runners from your existing strawberry plants (see p.135) if you wish.

Strawberries are perfectly happy in containers and raised beds, even grow bags and hanging baskets, but you'll need to keep particularly on top of watering and feeding to keep them moist but never waterlogged. Little and often is best.

Harvesting and storage

Depending on variety, you can harvest strawberries from May until October. Pick the berries when they are well coloured all over, preferably when the sun is hot, to really bring out the flavour and aroma of your fruit.

Strawberries don't freeze as well as other berries, but if you have a glut it's worth stashing some away for use in tarts, etc. Freeze them in a single layer on a tray so they don't stick together, tipping the fruit into a bag or container once frozen.

Pests and diseases

Birds can be a real pain and although scaring devices (like ribbons on a cane and spinning CDs) can help, netting is the only certain remedy.

Botrytis (see p.177) can affect strawberries, especially in a rainy summer. It's exacerbated by splashing the fruit as you water, so do take care. Keeping weeds down and ensuring that plants have plenty of air circulating around them is hugely helpful in minimising the likelihood of getting this tedious disease.

Blotchy and/or yellow leaves usually indicate strawberry virus especially if yields simultaneously decline. Once it arrives, pull up and incinerate any affected plants before it spreads.

Slugs and snails can be a nuisance, especially in wetter summers. Deal with them as you prefer (see p.180).

Eating

I rarely get too many strawberries into the house. If it's not me, then my wife or daughter will eat those that ripen each day in the sun. Strawberry jam is rightly popular, but I like to get the fresh berries into tarts and next to anything dairy.

Recipes Rhubarb and strawberry tart (p.240), Strawberry granita (p.243), Fruity melons (p.223) and Strawberry trifle (p.244). See also variations for cranachan (p.218), mess (p.224) and muffins (p.207).

Sourcing & Creating
your Plants

You can pick up a tree or bush for your garden from any

garden centre and the chances are it'll be just fine. Having got this far through the book though, I hope I've managed to dissuade you from settling for 'just fine'. With fruit this is crucial: if the varieties of potato you went for aren't too special, there's always next year's catalogues to peruse for alternatives, but most fruit will be with you far longer. Plant the wrong apple or quince tree and you and your ancestors may have a few hundred years to live with 'OK' fruit. It pays to get the choice right first off.

Sourcing plants

You wouldn't go into a plant nursery for light bulbs and door paint, so don't go to a home store for your plants. You're starting a long relationship with your plants, so show them a little love from the start and buy from people who raise them for a living. There are some wonderful nurseries and suppliers listed in the Directory (pp.248–9). I have used each of them over the years and they are all excellent. They know what they're doing, having built up expertise, knowledge and a reputation over many years. They care that your plants grow, and they hope you will come back for more.

Getting the best

For many fruits it pays to look nearby to find a nursery that specialises in local varieties. Apples, plums and pears are among the fruits that have endless varieties available and local cultivars are well worth considering, as a plant that has evolved in the soils, climate and with the seasonal variations you want to plant it in is very likely to grow happily and healthily. I'm fortunate to have Thornhayes a few miles away; I need go no further if I want an apple that originates from a pip-spitting distance away from my orchard. Look for a similar source near you, and if not go for one of the suppliers in the Directory (pp.248–9).

Of course, many types of fruit have only one (or just a few) available varieties, and some (like apricots) have a less busy history of cultivation in this country. However, there are usually some varieties of each that sit above the rest, and I have identified these in the Fruit A–Z (pp.28–121).

The less common varieties and the more unusual fruit are likely to be found with specialist nurseries. Check the Directory for these too.

If you possibly can, go to open days and Apple Day celebrations where you get the chance to try the fruit before you buy the plants. Check out the events at Brogdale (the home of the National Fruit Collection in Kent) as well as any venues closer to home.

Cordon gooseberries

Choosing rootstocks

Many fruit trees and some bushes are grown on roots from other plants. A young branch is taken from the parent plant of the variety you require (e.g. 'Ashmead's Kernel' apple) and grafted (i.e. joined) to a root system (known as a rootstock) specially grown for that purpose. The rootstock helps control the speed and extent of the plant's growth, and encourages many to fruit much earlier than they might otherwise. It also allows the plant to be grown in soils that the parent tree might not suit, and it can offer a degree of protection against some diseases.

Grafting plant material from a parent tree onto a rootstock will always result in a new plant of the same variety as the parent, so you always know what you are getting, whereas growing from seed can produce unpredictable results due to cross pollination. To avoid potential disappointment, I'd recommend going for grafted trees. It also means you get a tree that suits your taste and your available space.

Dwarfing rootstocks are increasingly available for fruit trees, often resulting in a tree no more than 1.3m in height and perfectly productive grown in a large pot.

Don't fret too much about the different types of rootstock. There's little need to remember the array of illogical letters and numbers that make up the names of most rootstocks. For the relevant fruit, I've outlined the commonest rootstocks but do let your nursery advise, based on your site and available space.

Choosing the shape: freestanding trees

Freestanding trees are, as the name implies, grown without support or a guiding structure. This usually means they are in a classic goblet, in order of increasing size: bush, half-standard or standard trees, and pyramid shape. Your choice of rootstock will guide the eventual size of each of these freestanding possibilities.

Bush trees These have a short trunk, 90cm at most, from which branches spread to form a low canopy.

Half-standard trees These are similar to bush trees, but with a taller trunk, usually about 1.5m, and consequently taller than most bushes, reaching 4–5m overall.

Standard trees The largest form, with 2m of main trunk and a large canopy. This form is suitable only for larger gardens and fields where you can access the crop.

Pyramid trees These are Christmas tree-shaped, tapering from short branches at the apex to wider spreading branches lower down. Sunlight can reach most of the tree, but it does take regular pruning to maintain the shape. Pyramids can also be grown (and maintained more easily) on dwarfing rootstocks. Spindlebushes are variations on pyramids, being shorter and often wider.

Freestanding tree shapes

Bush tree

Half-standard tree

Standard tree

Pyramid tree

Choosing the shape: trained forms

Trees can be grown in a range of shapes, from the classic tall pyramid to a 30cm-high single-branched stepover. Your choice of rootstock plays a role in determining the potential shapes open to you, but initial pruning is equally important. Many suppliers sell trees where this initial training has been either partially or fully carried out. With careful planning you'll be able to grow fruit trees even in a small space.

For many plants, there is the option of training them into a range of styles and shapes. I've identified these options for each fruit in the A–Z where this applies.

Some varieties are more suitable for training than others and spur-bearing varieties (see p.37) are usually best. Tip-bearers (those that produce fruit on the end of short sideshoots) would have their sideshoots pruned off if grown in most training styles. Most pears are suitable as they tend to be spur-bearers, while many apples are not. So, it pays to seek advice from a nursery as to the best varieties to suit your location and the training method you're considering.

Common trained options include:

Espaliers Grown flat against a wall and/or framework of wires, with three or four levels of evenly spaced horizontal branches growing either side of the vertical trunk. Apples and pears are particularly suited to being trained in this manner.

Fans Similar to espaliers, but the main trunk is short, with branches that radiate from the base of the plant rather than growing horizontally. This method suits many of the stone fruit and some currants and berries.

Stepovers Grown either as a low single cordon bent over to the horizontal or with a branch going both ways so that they resemble a low single-tiered espalier.

Cordons Most commonly single-stemmed trees grown at an angle of around 45°, usually against a wall and/or a wire supporting system. This is a particularly good method for squeezing a few trees into a small space. You may find double cordons for sale, where two main stems are trained into a U-shape or even a multiple cordon with three or four arms. Spur-fruiting varieties are needed (see p.37).

Minarettes are essentially cordon trees, grown vertically and not usually attached to wires. Also known as column, ballerina or leg trees, they can be planted close together (perhaps 60cm depending on variety).

If the idea of one of these trained shapes appeals, I'd recommend investing in a partially trained plant. Although more expensive than an untrained plant, buying one with the hard work done gets you off to a good start and nearer a harvest.

Trained tree shapes

Espalier

Fan

Stepover

Cordon

Creating your own plants

Creating your own plants is pretty straightforward, though it may seem intimidating at first. It usually means you'll be a little behind in harvesting than if you'd bought plants, but it's a good way of starting cheaply, or extending what you grow.

Cuttings

Taking cuttings can feel a little hit and miss but it is by far the simplest and most widely applicable way of creating new plants from old. Cuttings are usually taken using either hardwood at the end of the season's growth or soft new growth.

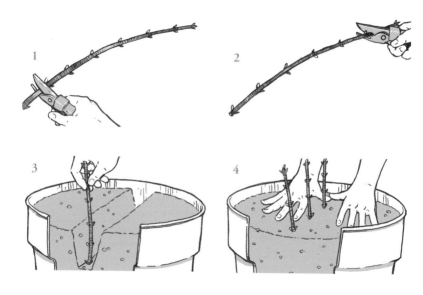

For hardwood cuttings In autumn or winter, prune at least half a dozen healthy 20cm lengths of this year's growth, cutting just below a leaf bud (1). Cut off any sideshoots. Using a sloping cut, snip off the top end of each cutting, just above a leaf bud (2). This ensures water and any leaking sap will drain away from the cut, and serves as a handy reminder of which way up the cutting is. Sink the cuttings into a pot filled with moist, well-drained compost (3) so that only one-third is above soil level. Firm cuttings in well (4), water and stand the pots in a light, sheltered, frost-free location over winter. It may be several months before hardwood cuttings take. Resist the temptation to pester them, and don't pot them on until new growth is well established.

For softwood cuttings Take several cuttings, about 10cm in length (1), early in the growing season as new growth appears. Using a sharp knife, cut just below a leaf joint at the base (2), slicing off all but two or three leaves at the top of the cutting, flush with the stem. Make holes in your compost around the rim of the container with a pencil and gently ease your cuttings in (3). Cover the cuttings with a clear plastic bag (food/freezer bags are ideal) using an elastic band or string to hold it in place (4) to keep the humidity up. Keep the pot in a bright spot but out of direct sunlight. Root development and subsequent growth are much faster than with hardwood cuttings but the delicate tissues are more liable to wilt.

Whichever type of cutting you are taking, a few rules are worth following:
- Whether using a knife or secateurs, the blade should be very sharp and clean.
- Take cuttings that have a minimum of two leaf nodes: the bottom one will form roots, the top one will form new growth.
- Unless taking cuttings from plants needing ericaceous conditions (such as blueberries), use special cutting compost mixed with grit for good drainage.
- Keep cuttings in a dry, sheltered, bright location but not in direct sunlight.
- Although the compost should be moist when you put the cuttings into it, you should keep watering to an absolute minimum (i.e. when the compost has dried out) until rooting has occurred.
- Using organic hormone rooting compounds can considerably increase your success rate.

Grafting

Grafting is a technique of joining the roots of one plant to a piece of wood of another (known as a scion) to produce a plant that will fruit true to the variety of the stem but tolerate the conditions and grow to the size imposed by the rootstock. It is an unreliable process as grafts can fail to take, some need extra heat and it's not without its fiddle but once you've grafted your first tree you may feel the urge to start your own nursery. It's as simple as choosing a new shoot and splicing it (in one of a few very particular ways) onto your chosen rootstock and sealing it until the graft has taken.

There are a few approaches but the simplest is the 'whip-and-tongue' method. For each tree you want, cut a length of the previous year's growth in December or January and store it in a fridge in a plastic bag to keep the wood dormant. This scion should be 5mm–1.5cm in diameter. Acquire a rootstock for each tree you require (see Directory, pp.248–9, for suppliers); the supplier can advise.

The graft should be made from February to April and must be done under cover, in a greenhouse, polytunnel or even your house. Take the scion with two to four buds and make a long diagonal cut away from you, through the scion, to create an exposed face 3–5cm long. The scion sloping cut is known as the 'whip'.

Then make a second cut starting a third of the way down the sloping cut: you are aiming for a cut almost parallel to the sloping cut, but not all the way through the wood, creating a 'tongue', so that a jagged 'Z' edge results. Make as near identical cuts as you can on the rootstock at a point where the diameter matches that of the scion, and join the two – they should slide snugly in together, held by the tongue of each.

This graft needs to be taped together to support it while the union takes. You can buy biodegradable grafting tape, although plastic tape or even masking tape

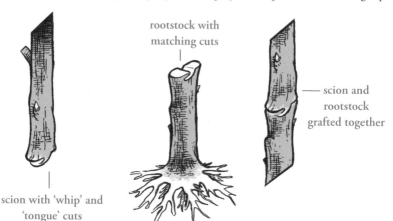

scion with 'whip' and 'tongue' cuts

rootstock with matching cuts

—— scion and rootstock grafted together

does a reasonable job, but you need to remember to cut the tape off in midsummer to avoid constricting growth.

Apples and pears are relatively easy to home-produce using grafting, but others (plums included) need additional warmth to succeed.

Layering

Many of the cane fruit, such as Japanese wineberries and blackberries, have evolved a marvellous strategy for colonising new ground: they produce new roots wherever their stems touch the soil. The enterprising grower can take advantage of this by simply organising this natural tendency to suit.

Choose a healthy shoot and strip off the leaves around 20cm from the shoot's tip (1). Bend the shoot to the ground and excavate a small groove in the soil where the bare part of the stem touches the ground. Make a small cut in the shoot's skin that will be in contact with the soil (in order to stimulate root growth), and use a bent piece of wire (or two) to hold the stem to the ground (2). Tie the rest of the stem with the growing tip to a short cane to keep it growing vertically (3). Bury the bald part of the stem in the groove and water well (4).

Once the plant has rooted, you can separate it from its parent with secateurs and pot on your new plant.

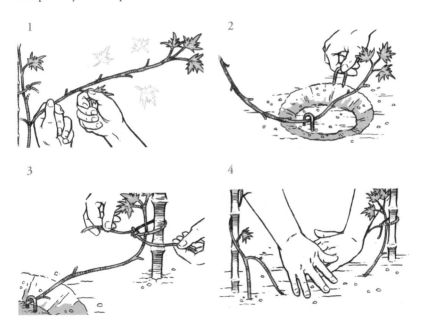

Divided, potted rhubarb plants

Division

Rhubarb can be divided to create new plants. As winter approaches you can split the core vertically into three of four pieces (depending on the size of the plant) using a spade, making sure each section has healthy roots and at least one dormant bud. You can be fairly forceful, if careful. Although this looks like a rather medieval approach, the established parent plant will be much happier afterwards. Pot each section up ready for planting out in early spring, or plant them out immediately.

Runners

Strawberries mainly spread laterally, throwing out long arms with mini-plants growing on them (1). Lift these up and you'll notice what look like short dry roots; these are merely waiting to come into contact with a suitable growing medium. All you have to do is to pin them with a piece of bent wire into a pot of compost (2) or against a bare patch of soil and wait. You can even sink this pot into the ground to help retain moisture. Within a month those roots should be growing happily, and you can separate the new plant from the parent in autumn, keeping it in the pot until planting out the following spring.

1
2

Suckers

Raspberries throw up stems from the base that can grow where you don't want them to, crowding out the other stems. These are known as suckers. If you carefully excavate around these and separate them from the base of the main plant, along with a reasonable amount of root system, you'll have a new plant to pot on or replant immediately.

Sowing

Compared to vegetables and herbs, not many fruits are best grown from seed. Melons and alpine strawberries are exceptions; refer to the A–Z entry on melons (p.83) for guidance on sowing and growing.

Planning, Preparation
& Planting

It can be very tempting to rush straight to the planting,

digging a hole and getting your plants into their new homes as quickly as possible, but resist the urge. If you spend some time planning and preparing, the planting will be simpler and your garden is likely to be more fruitful.

Planning your space

Find a piece of paper and a pencil and sketch out your garden, allotment, balcony or patio. Gently shade areas that have the least sun and mark any areas you want to keep clear for access, for eating or whatever else your space is called upon to provide. Take a moment to consider whether you are being realistic. The space dedicated to paths and other access is almost always underestimated, so be on the generous side.

Make a list of opportunities and constraints – access to sunshine, water, shelter or the degree of shade, wind and potential drought are all key factors, as is any perceived lack of space. Think about what you're hoping for from your space too, and list it: are you after maximum productivity regardless of aesthetics; are you hoping to encourage wildlife to your space; must it be beautiful, etc. The questions and responses will be yours alone. And don't be discouraged by what seems like a negative point, such as limited sunlight. Such constraints are often just signposts to a delicious edible solution. For example, 'Morello' cherries are perfectly fruitful on a north-facing wall and raspberries will tolerate some shade.

Your wish list of what you would like to grow in an ideal world and the Fruit A–Z (pp.28–121) will help you select potential candidates for your space but do take your time at this stage. Consider the suggestions below for the ways you can grow your fruit, look into container growing (see p.184) if you think that may be for you, and be happy with your plan before you get your hands dirty.

Preparation is frequently overlooked and planting often undertaken in a hurry, both of which can hold your plants back. Do both steps well and your plants have every chance of establishing and growing healthily. And if they do that, you will have fruit much sooner.

Fruit in a small space

Everyone wants more space. Even if you have a field the chances are you'd like another, but if you're genuinely limited for space, fear not, you'll be able to grow most fruit plants.

Dwarfing rootstocks are available for most fruit trees (see A–Z entries) and there are any number of ways of training plants against walls and/or wires to get a considerable harvest from an almost-flat plant.

Vertical planting is another wonderful way of laying your hands on some fruit without taking up much ground space. Grapes will happily climb up and over a structure, and some fruit (apples and pears in particular) can be grown in a narrow shape, even fruiting from a single main stem (see cordons, p.128). Nurseries are always coming up with varieties to suit growing in small spaces – it's a huge market. For example, there are now strawberry varieties that suit either growing downwards from hanging baskets or being trained vertically to take up little room. Keep your eyes out for tasty-sounding newcomers.

Container growing is a great way to go and there are a number of options and considerations you should be aware of (see pp.184–7).

Planning an orchard

The secret to creating a good orchard is in choosing the right mix of trees. You should be led by the different fruit you'd like to eat, certainly, but you'll need to consider pollination and spacing too. Are your trees self-fertile or will you be looking to plant compatible varieties? The key to getting things right on the ground is to make a plan to scale on graph paper, then mark it out on the ground with canes. Don't be tempted to squeeze trees closer together than they should be. They may look like lonely teenagers at their first school dance, but only for a few years while they establish. They'll make an orchard soon enough.

Growing in a fruit cage

Growing in a fruit cage

If you've been cleared out of a summer's precious harvest of currants or berries by the birds even once, you'll have let the idea of a fruit cage cross your mind. A metal or wooden frame, usually at least 2m tall, supports a netting fine enough to exclude birds while allowing pollinating insects through unimpeded. I'm no fan of netting when it comes to vegetables as it excludes you from the plants, can accidentally trap birds and is usually plain ugly, but fruit cages are entirely different. They create a room in which the plants can grow without the nuisance and allow through everything that is beneficial: light, care and you included.

Fruit cages aren't cheap to buy but, like a polytunnel, once up, their framework will last for years with only the occasional replacement or repair to the covering.

Allotment and garden growing

Most people will grow their fruit in a garden or at their allotment where it's likely that some plants are already grown. This is perfectly fine but requires a little forethought, notably whether to keep your fruit in its own separate area or integrate it with the other plants. Growing fruit in dedicated beds makes for a simple start-up, allowing you to prepare the whole area well (see p.142), ensuring it is free from grass and weed competition from the start. Take time to make a paper plan, as for an orchard, and similarly don't be panicked if it all looks a little sparse after planting – it'll look that way for a short time followed by years of fully grown productivity. Planting closer may look less empty early on, but as your plants grow they'll begin to crowd each other and the shade and competition for nutrients and space will reduce your harvests and encourage disease.

One way of finding room for fruit (and vegetables) is to grow them alongside ornamentals in the garden. With allotment waiting lists not getting any shorter and food prices increasing, those who want to grow some of what they eat are planting trees, shrubs, vines and smaller fruit wherever they can find a space. Lawns are shrinking and ornamentals are being replaced with good-looking edibles to get the best of both worlds. Again, be aware of how big plants will eventually become. And remember that there are many edibles (mint, for example) as well as ornamentals that prefer to be in the shade of a tree or bush.

Forest gardens

If you want to take the idea of integrating plants together to another level then a forest garden may be for you. These multi-level gardens take the home gardens of Kerala, India as their inspiration, planting some or all of the layers found in a young forest to make a productive whole. Layers span from underground tubers, through the herb, fungi and ground cover layer, up through shrubs and smaller plants to smaller trees and potentially a canopy later at the top. Climbing plants may crawl between each layer. In Europe it is rare for a canopy layer to exist, as it can severely limit the light that reaches lower tiers, limiting productivity in the process. The idea works on any scale, from acres down to a corner of a garden: you just select the uppermost layer where plants are typically largest that makes sense for your space. It takes careful planning and preparation but the main advantage of going for a forest garden is that once established it functions as a balanced ecosystem with minimal intervention from you. You'll probably need to plant more than just fruit to create a functioning forest garden but if it tickles your fancy, see the Directory (pp.248–9) for additional sources of information.

The aspect

Whether you're planning for an orchard or a fruit cage, integrating fruit into your garden or intending to grow your fruit in a collection of containers, the degree of exposure to harsh winds, to sunshine and the slope of the land – collectively, the aspect – will significantly affect how happy and productive your plants will be.

Generally speaking, fruit enjoys shelter, sun and heat, so look for a space that offers these. With the odd exception, you should give your sunniest spot to fruit.

Shelter is often the critical factor when it comes to fruit. Any exposure to harsh winds when flowering is happening can severely impair pollination rates, fruit set and, in turn, your harvest. If you haven't a sheltered spot, then consider planting some windbreak hedging. It's nowhere near as exciting as planting a peach or a mulberry but it may be the difference between eating the fruit and not.

Preparing the ground

Unless you are growing your fruit in containers, you'll need to spend a little time ensuring the soil is ready for your plants. The ideal is a soil with a fine tilth (i.e. in small, crumbly particles rather than large clods) to a depth below the bottom of the root system of the plants you are putting in. It should be free from weeds and grass and have a good level of nutrients to get the plants off to a healthy start.

Clearing any grass is vital as it can compete strongly with establishing plants and compromise their growth. If you have a few months before planting you can lay thick cardboard directly on top of the grass, keeping it in place with bricks. Over the course of a few months the cardboard will kill the grass and any weeds underneath, leaving a clean patch to plant into. Otherwise, strip off the top 7–10cm with a spade, leaving the turf somewhere to break down as it's very nutrient rich.

Whichever route you take, or if your ground was grass- and weed-free to begin with, dig over the area well and add compost or composted horse manure if you can – to give the soil a nutrient and humus boost before you plant.

Getting to know your soil

Fruit grows best in a fertile, deep soil – one that retains moisture to a degree but also drains well. You will need to get to know your soil. If it's in an ideal state then happy days. If not, don't be deterred – there is much you can do to nudge it towards the conditions you want.

Getting a professional analysis of your soil is simply a matter of posting a couple of trowelfuls to someone who offers the service and waiting a few days to receive their report. You'll learn about the texture, pH and nutrient status of your soil – all of which play a huge part in the livelihood and the quality of your fruit harvest. The information is accurate, reasonably detailed and not expensive for what you get, and (if you request it) you may well be given advice about how to improve any deficiencies.

I have to confess I didn't bother with soil testing when I started growing veg but as soon as I thought about planting fruit I had a soil analysis done. Trees aren't cheap, they are with you a long time and the investment really is worth it. Don't let yourself be intimidated by a little science. Taking a sample and understanding the results is a straightforward business and getting to know your soil pays dividends year after year, harvest after harvest.

If you prefer, you can also take a rough and ready approach and analyse the soil yourself (see below). This is certainly perfectly adequate if you are planting only a small area.

Soil texture Heavier, more water-retentive soils contain a large proportion of clay whereas at the other end of the spectrum you'll find the free-draining sandy soils. Somewhere in the middle are the loamy soils with a reasonably equal amount of sand and clay, capable of retaining some moisture while freely letting excess drain. This is the perfection that blesses few of us, so to move the soil nearer the ideal we need to examine our soil texture.

Take a good handful of soil and assess it. If it feels gritty and will crumble easily through your fingers you have a sandy soil. Moisten it a little and although it may form a cracked golf-ball-sized sphere it will refuse to roll into a sausage. These soils drain freely, warm up very quickly in spring and are easy to work for most of the year. All good news, but the sandiness creates air spaces which let precious water drain away rapidly in times when it might be needed, often taking valuable nutrients with it. This can lead to a dry soil that becomes increasingly acidic as the calcium is leached out, which in turn can limit the availability of the nutrients that remain. The soil becomes 'hungry', dependent on regular watering and feeds.

Clay's small particle size limits air spaces, meaning clay soils drain less readily than others, holding on to moisture and making them harder to dig and grow in.

Compost

They also tend to be easy to compact and slower to warm up in the spring. Grab a handful, moisten it and it will form a sphere easily and be happy to extend into a thin sausage shape. The ease with which these soils compact means that any extended period without rain leaves them hard and dry. They tend to be rich in nutrients, but without the air spaces for water to move about, these nutrients are often locked up and unavailable to plants.

Loams take the middle ground. Neither too sandy or clayey, they enjoy some drainage thanks to the sand, balanced with the moisture-retaining quality of the clay. They also have good nutrient levels, which the air spaces make readily available to growing plants. This is the happy medium, and if you have it, crack open a bottle of your favourite tipple and celebrate.

Chalky soils usually display their chalky lumps fairly obviously when dug. They're alkaline (see below) and usually shallow, which together can limit the choice of plants that will do well.

Other soil types are comparatively rare and either less than suitable for growing (thin moorland soils, for example) or famously productive (such as peat). You are unlikely to have these soils but if you do, then seek professional advice.

In most cases your key to moving towards (or maintaining) the perfect loam is the same: organic matter. Adding organic matter in the form of compost, as well as top-dressing with more compost and/or well-rotted manure in subsequent years, adds essential fibre and air spaces to clay soils, body and water retention to sandy soils, and dilutes the chalk component of a chalky soil.

Soil pH This is a measure of the relative acidity or alkalinity of your soil. As with soil texture, the majority of plants do well in a reasonably neutral soil, near the middle of the scale. There are some fruits (such as blueberries) which prefer something a little more extreme, and where this is the case, it's covered in the specific entry in the Fruit A–Z (pp.28–121).

The pH influences the availability of nutrients in the soil and can, for various reasons, often to do with solubility, prevent your plants accessing nutrients that are present. The results of a professional soil test will include a pH analysis and may offer advice about any action to take.

Many garden centres and other suppliers will sell a home pH testing kit that serves reasonably well too. It is simple to use one of these: put some soil in the tube supplied, add a few drops of test solution, shake and leave it to settle. After a few minutes you compare the colour of the sample with the colour chart supplied and read the result.

Most soils, especially in domestic gardens, will be somewhere towards neutral, neither strongly acidic nor alkaline. This is ideal. If your result indicates a soil that is strongly acidic you can neutralise the acid by applying an alkali. Agricultural lime (naturally occurring calcium carbonate) is the cheapest, most widely available form of lime for the grower and it can be applied at any time of the year, although best in late winter. It's easy to use: just throw it over the area you want to affect at the rate suggested on the packet. The result isn't instant as it needs to be incorporated into the soil, but it is effective and relatively cheap. It's also easy to find in garden centres, countryside suppliers or through specialist suppliers, but do make sure the lime comes from a sustainable source.

Strongly alkaline soils are extremely rare. They can, in theory, be acidified using sulphates but this is costly and environmentally damaging. If you are one of the unlucky few it's much better to dilute the alkalinity by incorporating as much compost, topsoil and well-rotted manure as you can lay your hands on. Your other alternative is to grow fruit in containers (see p.184).

Get to know your soil, make a few adjustments to counter any extremes of soil texture and pH if necessary, but don't strive too hard for the (often unattainable) holy grail of the perfect neutralish loam across the whole of your garden. Unless you are growing only a few types of fruit that enjoy very specific requirements, you should find that as long as you're away from the harsh extremities of texture and pH your plants will do pretty well.

In any event, while many plants prefer the soil to be just so, they are reasonably productive across a range of soil conditions either side of the ideal. And you can always add a little localised lime to those that like their soil slightly alkaline, and a little ericaceous compost around the roots of those that prefer things a touch more acidic.

Planting a tree

Planting a tree well is about a little more than just digging a hole to make room for the root ball of your plant. Do it properly and your tree will romp away happily, do it less well and you'll put a halt to healthy establishment that can take the tree some time to get over.

You can plant bare-root trees any time in the dormant season, from November to March, and pot-grown plants can be planted at any time of year. November is the ideal time for either, as the soil is still warm, allowing roots to start to become established before the winter dormancy begins. This means that in the following spring the trees grow away quickly. Note that bare-root trees should be kept in shallow soil until you are ready to plant them, so they don't dry out.

There will always be some difference of opinion about how best to plant and stake a tree – here are some tips that have worked well for me.

- Give your tree's roots a good pre-planting soak in a bucket of water.
- If you are planting into grassland or lawn, remove any turf so that you have at least 1m² of bare ground, even if your plant is considerably smaller in spread.
- Dig a hole 10cm or so below the depth that you'll need to plant the tree.
- Place a cane across the top of the hole and put the tree into the hole to check that the graft (if the tree has one) is at least 10cm above ground level and that the whole of the root system is below. If the tree has no graft, plant it to the depth it was in the pot, or if supplied as a bare-root plant, ensure the roots are completely below the surface of the soil.
- Whether pot-grown or bare-rooted, you should be able to tell from the trunk how deep the tree was grown at the nursery – plant it at the same depth.
- After checking that the depth of the hole and the position of the tree are correct, put the tree back in the bucket of water to keep the roots moist.
- Probably the most important part of planting is to loosen the sides and the base of the hole. Doing this improves drainage and ensures the hole doesn't act like a box, ready to fill with water in rainy periods. It also gives the roots broken earth to grow into rather than a wall of soil. The heavier and more clayey your soil, the more beneficial this is.
- I plant trees and many other plants with mycorrhizal fungi. Available as a powder or gel, these fungi work in symbiosis with the root system, bringing nutrients to the plant as they establish in the ground in exchange for a few of the plant's carbohydrates. It benefits the tree and stimulates healthy growth.
- Crumble handfuls of soil between the roots – into and under the centre of the tree. Aim to fill the heart of the root system with small soil particles, leaving no large air pockets.

- Break up the turf you removed from the surface into small pieces and lay it, grass down, in the bottom of the hole around the tree, then backfill with loose soil, treading in well.
- Thoroughly water immediately.
- I don't add compost and fertiliser when planting as I feel it entices the roots to stay where they are, in a reservoir of nutrients. Without that reservoir the roots have an incentive to grow away in search of more.
- When you stake you are aiming to secure the roots rather than prevent the tree from moving at all. To achieve this you only need to use a short 70cm stake with 40cm knocked into the ground – the 30cm above ground is tied to the tree with a rubber figure-of-eight loop. This secures the base of the tree, preventing the root system from being forced up in strong winds, but leaves the top to move in the wind, developing its own strength.

A newly planted tree: staked, mulched and guarded

Caring for your Plants

Fruit plants more or less take care of themselves. Almost all are perennial and once established they tend to grow away early each spring and can be productive for many years. Left to their own devices, they will give you a harvest more often than not, but if you are prepared to do a little to help them on their way you'll not only encourage a healthier tree, you'll likely as not end up with a far larger crop to take to the kitchen.

The ongoing tasks are pruning, watering, feeding and weed control. As with most things in the garden or the allotment, good timing for those once-in-a-while tasks is vital and anything you need to do more frequently, such as watering, is best undertaken little and often.

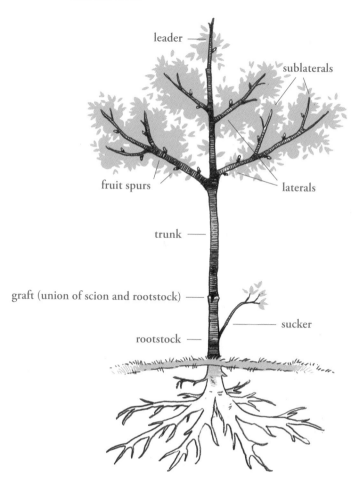

Pruning

Pruning is the art of removing plant growth to help shape your plant, maximise your harvests and minimise the threat of disease. Unpruned, most fruit would survive reasonably well and produce something to eat, but to maintain a healthier, long-lived, more happily cropping plant you'll need to prune.

Pruning helps to guide the plant into a shape you want; to reduce, train or encourage growth and fruiting; and to remove dead, congested, damaged or diseased wood. If you leave them to develop of their own accord, many plants will grow too congested, with closing, rubbing or densely packed branches. This stops good air flow and light penetration, encouraging disease and damage. Pruning to remove affected branches opens up the centre of the plant to air and light, helps prevent disease getting in through damaged tissue, and encourages vitality and health for the whole plant.

Pruning also reduces the volume of top growth, meaning that the roots don't have to work so hard to service the leafy, woody growth. In effect, this leaves a surplus of energy which the plant can use to produce seeds and fruit. If, in taking off some of the top growth, you do it in such a way as to leave the growth that has the best chance of giving you fruit, you'll be killing two birds with one stone – and that's the essence of much good pruning.

If you're new to it you may find the idea of pruning a little daunting. I did when faced with my first fruit trees that I knew I had to tackle one way or another. You may even convince yourself out of it by telling yourself that plants aren't pruned in their natural habitat, they're allowed to grow as they wish. This may be true, but the plant you have for your garden is being grown to give you the healthiest, largest (hopefully) crop of delicious fruit. And it is likely to have been bred – or at the very least selected – for domesticated growing. Pruning is part of the cycle of interaction between you and the plant that ensures it pays its edible rent every year.

Pruning isn't difficult. It is particular though, and rather than all plants being pruned the same way, each has its preferred treatment. It's simply a matter of knowing what to do when. Rhubarb, melons and strawberries will excuse you with a tidy-up rather than pruning as such, but the rest need a little more attention. Read carefully and take this book with you to the trees.

Some plants should only be pruned if absolutely necessary, while others will quickly reduce their harvest if you don't get busy with the secateurs. Specific advice is given for each entry in the Fruit A–Z (pp.28–121), but there are some general principles it's worth familiarising yourself with.

That said, if you forget or miss a year of pruning the plant is unlikely to die but please do, at the very least, keep a watch for crossing, dead or damaged branches and snip these out as this will help minimise the likelihood of diseases.

Pruning tools

Secateurs are a must, a penknife desirable, and a pruning saw and loppers vital if you are growing trees and larger shrubs. Go for the best you can afford (see p.22).

When to prune

The ideal time to prune varies with each fruit. Most of the fruit we grow in the UK prefers to be pruned in the dormant period through winter, with some happier to be pruned in the hotter months: the A–Z explains the details for each fruit and the chart on pp.32–3 should help you plan when to do your pruning.

How to prune

Before you pick up your tools, take a piece of chalk and mark the branches you are thinking of removing or shortening. After every major cut, stand back and see if you are moving towards the desired shape. Next decide whether secateurs are comfortably up to the task (i.e. if the branch is 1cm across or less), if not use loppers or a saw. This ensures the best chance of a clean cut.

Place the branch or stem in the centre of the blades rather than close to the pivot or near the tip. Never twist the tool – it will tear the cut, leaving rough edges where disease can more easily take hold. If you're tempted to twist, it usually means you should use a larger tool for the job – so stop and use a larger tool for the job.

If you are cutting off part of a stem, you'll want to cut about 6–8mm above a bud. You do this for two reasons: growth hormones are concentrated around buds

Chalk-marked branches, ready for pruning

Pruning to an outward-facing bud

and these hormones encourage rapid healing as well as new growth. Cutting just above the bud gives the plant minimal exposure to disease and ensures that new growth from this bud takes over the main growth of this stem. The choice of bud is important. New growth occurs in the direction the bud faces, and usually you want to encourage new growth outwards, away from the heart of the plant. This avoids overcrowding and gives the stems a better chance of getting good light.

The angle at which you make your cut depends on how the plant produces its buds. If they are in pairs on opposite sides of the stem then cut straight across about 6mm above the pair of buds. If the buds are borne singly (usually spread along the stem) then make an angled cut of around 30° sloping back from the bud, as this minimises the likelihood of water or sap collecting on the cut surface, helping it heal more quickly. Whichever type of cut you make, use a tool with a sharp blade as a smooth cut heals well and lessens the opportunity for disease to get in.

Pruning a freestanding tree

A freestanding tree (as opposed to one that's been trained into an espalier, etc) is the most common form of tree. Most nurseries can supply a tree that will take perfectly happily to being grown as a freestanding tree but you may have to do a little early pruning, known as formative pruning, to guide it into shape. Once established, routine pruning is needed to keep your tree healthy and productive. Freestanding trees are grown as bushes, half-standards, standards and pyramids.

Bush, half-standard and standard trees These are pruned into a goblet shape, where a ring of branches defines an open centre, allowing light and air into the heart of the tree. This promotes good health, minimises disease and ensures that developing fruit have the conditions they like to grow well.

If you have bought a maiden whip (a one-year-old tree with a single long trunk and no side branches), you'll need to cut this to the height where you'd like the side branches to develop. You may be supplied a tree that's a year older where this first step has already been carried out. Whether bought at this latter stage or created from a maiden whip, the side branches (laterals) should be at a wide angle to the trunk and will form the core shape of your bush or standard tree. The next formative steps are simple.

For apples and pears the timings are as follows:
- First winter After planting your tree in winter, prune the central leader to a bud that's around 25cm above the highest lateral. Cut back the laterals by half, 6mm or so above an outward-facing bud. Remove any other branches that develop along the trunk. These are the most important cuts you'll make as this gives you the main structure from which your tree develops.

- **Second winter** Prune the laterals by one-third, each to just above an outward-facing bud, to encourage an open centre to the tree. Sublaterals will have grown from the laterals: choose three on each branch that aren't facing into the centre of the tree, as equally spaced as possible, and cut them back by a third. Shorten other sublaterals to three or four buds to encourage them to develop into fruiting spurs. Again, remove any shoots that have grown along the trunk.
- **Third winter** Choose further well-placed sublaterals to prune back by one-third to extend the network of branches, and prune back others to form short spurs of three or four buds as before. Remove any branches that are crossing or growing towards the centre of the tree.

Follow this process and your tree should have a good frame of laterals, each with a few sublaterals, and have formed a goblet shape. Pruning from this point follows a winter-only routine that is different for spur-bearing fruit and tip-bearing fruit.

Spur-bearing fruit This type of tree carries its fruit in clusters on short branches known as spurs. Fruiting spurs are at least 2 years old. Each winter cut back laterals by one-third, and prune sublaterals to leave four or five buds on each – this encourages new spurs to form, which will eventually fruit. Then prune off old, crowded or weak spurs, to leave at least 10cm or so between spurs.

Tip-bearing fruit This type of tree carries its fruit mainly on the ends of shoots produced the previous year. Each year you should prune out 25 per cent of the oldest branches and look to keep an open centre to the tree. Then prune back the tips on the remaining branches and snip out any shoots growing from the base. Over time, this method of pruning refreshes the whole top growth and ensures new productive fruiting branches.

For plum trees the timings are as follows:
- **First spring** Cut back the laterals by half, 6mm or so above an outward-facing bud. Remove any other branches that develop along the trunk, and cut back the central leader to just above the highest lateral. These are the most important cuts, giving you the main structure from which your tree develops.
- **Second spring** Sublaterals will have grown from the laterals. Choose three or four on each branch that are not facing into the centre of the tree, as equally spaced as possible, and cut them back by one-third. Remove any other sublaterals along with any shoots that have grown along the trunk.

The other stone fruit (cherries, peaches, nectarines and apricots) follow the process as for plums with any variations noted in their A–Z entry.

Pyramid trees These have the classic Christmas tree shape, with branches gradually shortening towards the top. The primary aim of pruning is to ensure space between fruiting branches so that light and air can get in and allow fruit to develop well. If your tree wasn't supplied already trained into a pyramid for you, make sure you buy a feathered maiden (see p.26) from which you can create a strong framework with the desired shape. It's very simple – although timing varies with different fruit (see relevant entries in the A–Z).

For apples and pears the timing is as follows:
- First winter Immediately after planting or during the first winter, shorten the leader to a strong bud around 75cm above the ground, and prune any good laterals by two-thirds to downward-facing buds. Prune off any weak or crowding laterals. You are aiming for a well-spaced network of branches.
- First summer Late in the summer new laterals will be apparent, mainly towards the top of the tree. Prune all of these new laterals back to five leaves.
- Second winter Cut back any of this year's growth to leave around 25cm of new growth.

With your pyramid shape established, routine winter pruning should aim to maintain the shape and healthy fruiting by pruning back the central leader to five new buds and thinning crowded spurs (leaving them no closer than 12cm apart). You can also cut out older branches and shoots to ensure good spacing and promote new growth. Each summer you should also prune back new laterals to around five leaves, and any sublaterals to three leaves, aiming to maintain the pyramid shape.

For pyramid plum trees the timings are as follows:
- First spring Starting with a feathered maiden, cut the central leader off at 1.5m or so with an angled cut. Remove any laterals lower than 0.5m and prune back the rest by half to an outward-facing bud.
- First summer Cut back main laterals to about 20cm of this year's growth, to a downward-facing bud.
- Second spring Prune back the central leader to a third of last year's growth.

In subsequent springs, cut back the central leader of your plum by two-thirds of last summer's growth until it reaches the required height. Each summer, once established, prune the leader back to 2–3cm of last summer's growth, and prune the upper branches to retain the Christmas tree shape. Remove any diseased, dead or damaged wood as well as any unproductive wood from congested areas.

The other stone fruit (cherries, peaches, nectarines and apricots) follow the process as for plums with any variations noted in their entry in the A–Z section.

Pruning trained fruit trees

Pruning trained fruit trees isn't tricky but it is very specific, so read carefully and if necessary take this book with you when you prune.

Espaliers These are essentially trees grown flat against a wall and/or framework of wires, with horizontal branches growing either side of the vertical trunk. Espalier training is particularly suited to apples and pears. It's usual for branches to be spaced around 40cm apart.

If you like the idea of an espalier tree then buy one already trained. It will be more expensive than an untrained tree but this reflects the time and effort taken in getting the tree to its initial shape and the amount of trouble it'll be saving you. If you want to do it for yourself, buy a maiden whip (i.e. an unbranching year-old tree). Set up your wire framework (either against a wall or freestanding) with the lowest wire 45cm or so from the ground and spacing further wires above 45cm or so apart. Plant your tree 5cm or so in front of the wires.

Prune your espalier tree as follows:

- First winter After planting your tree in winter, prune the central leader to just above the lowest wire.
- First spring In early spring, as new growth emerges, choose two good shoots under, but near the wire. These will grow into the first pair of horizontal branches.
- First summer Tie canes to these two growing shoots and tie them to the wires at an angle of 45°. Prune any sublaterals back to five leaves; remove any other shoots from the trunk. At the end of summer, untie the canes from the wires and laterals, bend the laterals down to the bottom wire and tie them to it.
- Second winter Prune the central leader to just above the second wire up, and prune the first pair of horizontals back by one-third to encourage good growth and fruiting spurs.
- Second summer Tie canes to two new growing shoots and follow the pruning advice for the first summer.

Repeat this process until your espalier has reached the desired height.

Ongoing routine pruning involves pruning sublaterals back to three leaves and any weaker growth to a single bud each summer, and thinning out spurs to 10cm or more between each.

Fans Fan-training suits many stone fruit, including peaches, apricots, cherries and some plums, as well as figs. It works best against a wall where these fruit benefit from the extra warmth and residual heat offered by the building. As with espaliers,

Fan-trained plum tree

fan-trained trees use horizontal wires (spaced 30cm or so apart) to support them but rather than grow horizontally, the branches themselves are trained across the wires into a fan shape, radiating roughly from the centre. The other key difference is that the initial branches (laterals) and some of the branches that come from them (sublaterals) both form the fan. Again, I'd suggest you buy trees that are at least partly trained as it takes around 4 years to train the tree into shape yourself. If you want to do this all for yourself, on the other hand, here are the steps to take.

- **First spring** After growth has commenced, prune off all but two shoots, which should be 30cm or so above the ground (where the first wire coincides with the trunk). Tie these two shoots outwards, either side of the centre at an angle of about 30° to the horizontal. Snip the leader down to the base of these two laterals. This is the core of your fan, from which all other branches will grow.
- **First summer** Select two sublaterals growing above and one below each lateral, and tie them to canes, which are in turn tied to the wire framework. Aim to establish a spreading hand of branches either side of the short trunk. Cut any other shoots back to one leaf.
- **Second spring** Prune the end of each branch (whether sublateral or lateral) by one-third to a bud facing the direction you want growth to continue in. This will encourage fruit-bearing spurs to develop. Remove any shoots growing into or out from the wire framework, along with any on the trunk below the laterals or crowding the centre.

Each year repeat the last two stages (first summer and second spring), adding canes and tying in new sublaterals until you have a well-balanced fan across the space you have available for it.

Once you have this structure in place, your pruning is very much more about encouraging new fruiting buds to develop. This involves stimulating new shoots to grow to replace old ones that have fruited. It is a simple process. Late in summer, prune off the shoots that have produced fruit and snip the shoots you have chosen to replace them back to three leaves to encourage new buds to develop, then tie them in. Keep up with this routine pruning or fruiting will slow dramatically.

Cordons Cordon trees are single-stemmed trees usually grown at an angle of around 45°, generally against a wall or a wire supporting system. This single main stem grows short fruiting spurs along its length, and growing at this angle allows you a greater harvest. You can grow them singly or (as many do) in greater numbers to get a hefty harvest from a relatively short space. Buy them with formative pruning already done for an easy life. Otherwise get a feathered maiden (see p.26), plant it at 45°, with the trunk attached to a cane.

That winter prune any laterals back to around four buds, just above an outward-facing bud. The following summer prune laterals back to three leaves and sublaterals to one leaf; fruiting spurs will result.

Ongoing routine pruning is simple. Each midsummer, prune laterals back to three leaves to form fruiting spurs and cut sublaterals back to just one leaf. This keeps a good balance of leaves while removing those not needed for good fruiting. Each winter, thin fruiting spurs to a minimum of 10cm from each other and prune back the leader in late spring.

Minarettes and stepovers These are pruned as for cordons.

Pruning soft fruit
Most soft fruit requires some pruning to maintain its health and productivity. As the method tends to vary for different fruit, this is covered in the A–Z entries.

Watering

Any plant is likely to get hungry and thirsty, even more so if it produces fruit. As plants get older, larger and more established, their developed root system can usually find plentiful water apart from during extended dry periods, but while a plant is getting established the level of care you give it can make the difference between surviving and thriving.

After planting, most fruit plants require frequent watering to help them through the establishment phase. How long and how much depends on the size of the plant but equally important is when it was planted. If you plant in autumn, as most nurseries recommend, almost all plants will be established by the time growth starts again in spring. Occasional watering during dry periods through the winter is the most you are likely to have to do.

Fruit planted in winter and spring (or later if pot-grown) will be trying to get its root system established while putting on new season's growth above ground in warming temperatures, so you will be required to give your hard-working plant water when the weather doesn't. Fruit planted in spring should ideally be watered throughout the first growing season when there is any period of dry weather.

Established trees rarely need watering other than in severe drought conditions. Strawberries have shallow roots and are particularly vulnerable to drying out, so do prioritise if you are growing them. Good mulching of strawberries is vital to help retain water and minimise the need for using the watering can. All other fruit will thank you for a soak once a week if it hasn't been raining, and more frequent drinks are a good idea for any plants near a wall or in containers.

Comfrey flowering

Maintaining health and fertility

A fruiting plant expends a vast amount of energy producing its fruit – or rather the seeds within it. Naturally, the typically large root system drives into the soil in search of nutrients, but you'll enjoy a heftier harvest if you make life a little easier for it. A combination of composted horse manure and/or compost around the base of the plant in the winter and potassium-rich feeds through the growing season will pay dividends when fruiting time arrives. You may well have to call on other sources of nutrients too.

Comfrey and liquid feeding

Once flowering begins it's also a good idea to keep topping up the nutrient bank. Many gardeners use seaweed and tomato feeds for their fruit – these are high in potassium, the essential nutrient required for healthy fruiting. Both are diluted in a watering can before use. Better still, you can make your own potassium-rich feed using comfrey.

You'll find comfrey, with its small pinky-white bell flowers and long, rough leaves, on many riverbanks. It looks very much like a borage plant that's enjoyed a good night out. Although far from unattractive, comfrey's real value lies in its capacity to accumulate minerals and nutrients. Deep-rooting, it scours the lower tiers of the soil horizon to bring precious potassium, phosphorus and nitrogen to the surface. It also grows rapidly. All you have to do is cut armfuls of leaves through the summer, which you can use in a variety of ways. Lay them, just cut and torn up, as a mulch around the base of your fruit plants and as they break down their nutrients will leach gently into the soil for the plants to take up as they need. Alternatively, you can incorporate them, torn up, into your compost bin where they act as an accelerator, driving compost-making rapidly onwards.

Both are fabulous ways of employing comfrey but I use almost all of mine as a liquid feed. Making your own is simple. Place torn-up leaves in an old onion net and suspend it in your water butt. Over the following weeks the leaves will decompose (the net stops sludgy bits blocking the tap) to create comfrey tea. You'll know when it's ready as it'll smell like an anchovy's plimsoll. Rough as it is, you will learn to love the stench, just a little, as it means a free boost to your fruiting plants, and more fruit for you. Just water it on or spray the leaves any time from when flowering begins. If you do not have a water butt or don't need very much, you can either use the same approach (with fewer leaves) in a watering can or chop the bottom off an upturned water bottle and fill it with leaves, using half a brick or similar to keep the leaves under pressure. Over the next 10 days or so a dark liquid will ooze from the leaves into the neck of the bottle. To use it, undo the lid and dilute the treacly liquid 15:1.

Comfrey leaves

Giving fruit plants a fortnightly feed is very effective in promoting health and good fruiting – better still to apply every other feed as a spray for the leaves. The leaves take in the nutrients quickly, not only making the leaves themselves healthier but also driving the nutrients rapidly into the plant's system with little waste. You will use less too.

Unless you have plenty of room to allow wild comfrey to grow, you'll want to source the Bocking 14 variety (see Directory, pp.248–9, for suppliers), as it's a sterile variety that doesn't set seed so you can easily control its spread. Expanding your comfrey bed is simple. Either divide the roots vertically with a spade, or dig the root up and chop across it to make slices like pound coins then grow these in pots until they're a good size to plant out.

You can follow the same method to make nettle tea, which is rich in nitrogen. This is ideal for stimulating green growth, so use it when that's what you want to encourage.

Making your own liquid feed like this saves money as well as the resources involved in creating bought feeds. Once you start growing a small patch of comfrey, you'll learn to love it as much as the fruit it feeds. It's an easy-to-grow, natural cut-and-come-again way of adding vital nutrients while you water that makes the fruit garden more self-reliant in nutrients. And those flowers provide the bees with a party venue, which means you have plenty around for the pollination your trees will require. And it's pretty much free.

Slow-release fertilisers

I'm not a fan of adding bought-in nutrients. I can live with adding composted horse manure, as it's usually locally available and puts a waste product to wonderful use, but I'm not one for throwing man-made/chemical fertilisers around. Most are made using fossil fuels, much water and even more energy, turning the simple energy-giving wonder of growing food into an energy- and carbon-heavy process. However, there are low-carbon alternatives.

Of the various options, I prefer organic pelleted chicken manure. High in the essential nutrients of nitrogen, potassium, phosphate and calcium, as well as many trace elements, the pellets are dried manure in an easy-to-use form that can be scattered around or dug into the growing medium. The pellets gently break down and dissolve, releasing their goodness for the plant to take up over an extended period. Follow the instructions on the packaging for frequency and amount to use. Look for a supplier using manure from chickens kept in free-range conditions (see Directory, p.249).

Compost

Compost is the secret of organic growing. Plant or sow something and chances are you'll have a reasonable first harvest, but without compost you're likely to see that fine start decline. Creating fruit is a hungry business for your plants and you'll need to put some of those nutrients into the equation if you don't want your soil to become depleted and the plants unproductive. Manure and liquid feeds are excellent sources, but compost has the added pleasure of turning waste that might otherwise make it to landfill into something that feeds the soil – and you and your family in turn. It closes a circle and makes it a cycle.

As an all-round plant fitness treatment, it's hard to beat compost. It replenishes nutrients, helps retain moisture, improves soil structure and makes a fine mulch. It is the cornerstone of organic growing and it's perfectly simple to make your own.

Making a compost bin While you don't need a bin to make compost (you can do it just in piles), it is far more practical to use one. Plastic bins are neat and easy to manage, but you can make your own. The most basic structure is a square of pallets lashed together, with the front able to be opened for access. It works well, especially to get you started. As your requirements grow, you can always replace it with more substantial bins. They're not expensive or time-consuming to make: you only need some wood, a saw, a hammer and nails. And they are more aesthetically pleasing.

Three adjacent bins are ideal. This is because turning the waste is the key to effective, rapid compost-making. Having bins next to each other makes turning easy and gives you the capacity to keep compost at different stages of decomposition separate from each other.

The process is simple: the first bin is the only one you add waste to. When it's full you turn it into the second bin and continue adding new waste to the first bin. Turning the compost in bin 2, watering each time, accelerates decomposition, so do it as often as you can. When bin 1 becomes full, turn the contents of bin 2 into bin 3, and bin 1 into the now-empty bin 2. Use the compost in bin 3 when ready; it will look and feel crumbly and (apart from a few twigs) be well broken down.

Pick a level, well-drained sunny spot for your bin(s), preferably on top of soil to allow excess water to drain, worms to get in, and the warmth of the sun to accelerate decomposition. If you can't site it on soil, add a base layer of soil or compost to ensure worms and beneficial organisms are present in the mix from the start.

At almost every course I run at River Cottage, someone tells me they can't make compost. They can. It's a perfectly natural process, but one that is often inadvertently halted by sealing the waste from the air. Throw on a binful of grass clippings and you won't have to wait long for it to turn to a slimy layer that will act like cling film, excluding air and halting decomposition. To make good compost all you have to do is avoid excluding the air and keep a reasonable balance of Greens to Browns (see below). There is nothing you need to do to force composting, it wants to happen anyway. Your job is to encourage the conditions for decomposition to happen efficiently. The secret lies in the mix of ingredients, and a little forethought really helps you get to grips with making fine compost.

Suitable materials for your compost bin:
Think of the ingredients as belonging to one of two groups: the Greens and the Browns. The Greens tend to be rich in nitrogen, and many are activators that nudge the Browns into quicker decomposition.

The main Greens include:
• Diluted urine (half a pint of urine to a gallon of water if you're asking)
• Grass cuttings
• Nettles
• Comfrey leaves

Other Greens that can be included:
• Raw vegetable peelings
• Tea bags and coffee grounds
• Young annual weeds (but avoid weeds with seeds at all costs)
• Unwoody prunings
• Animal manure (see p.167) from herbivores such as cows and horses (organic is ideal)
• Poultry manure and bedding

While often low in nutrients, Browns are rich in carbon. They decompose more slowly than Greens, but accelerate when composted with green activators.

The Browns include:
- Waste paper – shredded or torn
- Cardboard
- Bedding from omnivorous pets (such as rabbits)
- Tough hedge clippings
- Woody prunings – shredded or chopped
- Old bedding plants
- Sawdust and wood shavings
- Bracken
- Fallen leaves

Your compost bins will take much of what you and your garden have no need of but there are some waste products that you should very definitely leave out. Meat, fish, dairy and cooked food (including bread) are an invitation to pests, especially rats. Cat litter and dog faeces are a definite no-go. When it comes to perennial weeds and diseased plants, I generally incinerate them and add the ashes to the compost bin.

Wood shavings and shreddings are great as a weed-suppressing mulch but they can lock up valuable nitrogen, so it's best to keep them away from the base of your plants. You can put them into your compost but they can take longer to break down than many of the other ingredients in your bin, so add only in small quantities and with green activators, or let them break down for a year or two first. Avoid using any wood that has been treated with preservatives.

Even a thrown-together pile that has been lazily cared for will eventually decay, so it can be used as a fertiliser, but to make really good compost without an interminable wait there are some considerations.

Golden rules for making your own compost:
- Use more or less equal volumes of Greens and Browns but for your own mix take into account your site, the weather, the time you're able to put into it. Learn from your experiences, and remember...
- Greens and Browns regulate each other: if your compost is too wet, add more Browns; too dry, add some Greens.
- Don't use too thick a layer of either – the best compost is made when Greens and Browns are well integrated.
- Use green activators like grass cuttings to activate otherwise slow-rotting Browns.

- You can use the tougher Browns – in combination with the Greens they provide essential bulk and structure to your finished product. If you maximise their surface area by chopping or shredding you'll find the accelerating Greens will nudge tougher Browns along and you can always fish them out and put them into bin 1 again if you need to.
- Ideally, have three bins side by side and keep them turning and well watered.

Your compost should be ready to use after around 9 months but if you're feeling determined it can be yours in as little as 2 months. The principles are the same as for making any compost, but the key is in getting air and water into the mix and getting the waste in small pieces before you add it to the bin. Depending on the grade and volume of material you have to compost, use a chipper, shears or a mower to shred your material before adding it to the heap – this creates a greater surface area for decomposition to take place.

The more you mix your compost, the more air is incorporated. This generates heat as decomposition proceeds, which in turn speeds up the process. And as you turn your compost, water it well. Even better, pee on it... being careful of any nettles you may have added.

After a week or two the heap should be starting to warm up – plunge your hand into the centre to test. Warmth is good: it's telling you that decomposition is under way. Keep turning and peeing and it may get properly hot in the centre. Following on from a neighbour who successfully baked a jacket potato overnight in the centre of his compost bin, I 'hard-boiled' an egg in mine in a few hours this summer... I need to get out more.

If the compost starts to cool you'll need to turn it again, adding more water or urine if it's dry, or more material if it is too damp. Full-on warm composting will follow. You can repeat this a few times but eventually the heating effect will diminish. The heap can now be left to finish off by itself.

Whether you go for the speedy version or the more relaxed approach to compost-making, as the ingredients break down they will reduce in volume to produce a chocolate-coloured blend that's sweet-smelling and earthy. It may have more lumps and twiggy bits than garden-centre compost, but that's often the case. Bash up any larger lumps, and if there are any bigger twigs, snap them up and return them to bin 1 to compost some more.

Compost can be added to your garden or around the base of plants at any time of the year, but I tend to add most of mine in winter to ensure the plants are well set up for the growing season to come. Some like to incorporate their compost into the soil by digging it in during late winter or early spring but if you're a fan of the no-dig approach or prefer an easier life you can add compost as a mulch and allow the rain and earthworms to take the nutrients and organic matter into the soil.

Other sources of nutrients

With your own compost and comfrey to call on, your fruit plants should have a good bank of nutrients to keep them on top form. If you find that you need more, or that practical considerations make compost-making and comfrey tea impractical, there are other sources of organic matter you can add.

Horse or farmyard manure This is usually reasonably easy to source and is one of those pleasurable commodities which is a nuisance waste product to the owner and gold to the person taking it away. Everybody wins. High in essential nutrients and fibre, manure releases its goodness gradually into the soil as the winter rain and worm action take effect. Gently, over the whole year, the benefit of a layer of composted manure ringed around the roots (but not touching the trunk) will feed the tree and do much to give it the reserves to grow healthy, plentiful fruit. Make sure any horse manure you use has composted well – for a year is usually best. You should also ensure that the horses' bedding is straw; wood shavings may rob nutrients from the manure and the soil it is applied to as they break down.

Chicken manure Although very high in nutrients, this can be too harsh for your plants if applied neat, so it's best to add it to your compost to dilute it.

Seaweed This is very high in potassium. Small-scale harvesting (the odd carrier bagful) is a fantastic option if you live near the sea. All you need to do is rinse it clean of salt, before laying it on the ground around your plants or mixing into your compost bin.

Adding horse manure around rhubarb

Borage

Companion planting

This is the art of growing plants together, or in close proximity, so that one or both benefit from their relationship. It can take a number of forms:

• Attracting beneficial insects
• Repelling pests
• Accumulating minerals and/or fixing nitrogen for neighbouring or subsequent crops
• Disguising the scent of crops vulnerable to pests that navigate by their sense of smell
• Acting as a sacrificial plant; i.e. to attract pests away from the main crop and its fruit
• Providing physical help, such as shelter and support
• Acting as a natural fungicide

While nitrogen-fixing plants (see Green manures, p.171) are excellent ways of maintaining essential nutrient levels, companion planting may be more useful for fruit in attracting beneficial insects. For the organic fruit and vegetable grower, attracting insects that will help to keep potential pests in check makes an inexpensive, environmentally friendly and often beautiful first line of defence against trouble.

Flowers are the key. Early-flowering plants provide a picnic for the first bees and other pollinating insects, while others flowering through the growing season will not only keep pollination rates up, they'll attract a range of natural predators, such as ladybirds, that will feed on your aphids and other pests. Diversity of plants leads to diversity of insects and other organisms, promoting a natural balance that's more resilient to harm.

Some of the aromatic herbs – mint and lemon balm in particular – are thought to act as a natural fungicide by exuding essential oils. I'm unaware of any scientific proof of this, but many growers I know observe it working and underplant all their fruit trees. The choice is yours.

The principle of growing in tiers (see Forest gardens, p.141) allows you to use your fruit to both offer support to and receive support from other plants. Taking advantage of a tree (fruiting or not) to grow a grapevine through while planting shade-tolerant plants beneath is one example. In this way three harvests may be enjoyed from one location. While the grapes clamber through the fruit tree, lettuces may be grown beneath, with the shade preventing them from bolting (growing quickly to seed) in midsummer while still allowing them enough light to grow steadily. These partnerships are there for you to dream up and try, obviously within the limits of what the plant requires to thrive.

As well as some of the more general happy partnerships you can create for and with your fruit plants, there are some companionships that deliver very specific benefits for particular fruit. The following table includes some that I think work particularly well.

Companion	Companion for	Acts by
Basil	Apricots, nectarines and peaches	Releasing aromatic insect-repellent from its foliage
Umbellifer herbs, such as fennel, coriander, dill and parsley	Any fruit	Attracting natural predators, such as hoverflies and wasps (the nectar feeds them), which in turn prey on aphids, caterpillars and other pests
Mexican marigold (*Tagetes minuta*)	Woody fruit plants, such as Japanese wineberries	Suppressing weed germination
Lemon balm, oregano and mint	Most fruit, stone fruit especially	Releasing aromatic insect-repellent from its foliage
Comfrey	Any fruit	Deep-rooting mineral accumulator, high in potassium. Flowers early and loved by bees
Garlic	Raspberries	Repelling aphids
Borage	Strawberries	Increasing yields
Nasturtium	Apple	Climbing through the tree, repelling codling moth
Nasturtium	Melons	Attracting aphids away from the melons – a sacrificial crop
Alliums, i.e. onions, chives, garlic and leeks	Apple	Preventing apple scab (when established)
Hyssop	Grapes	Stimulating growth

Green manures

A group of plants that can greatly improve the health of your garden, allotment or even a group of pots. They achieve this by doing one or more of the following:

* Rooting deeply, aerating the soil and helping to break up heavy ground
* Taking nitrogen from the air, making it available in the soil to neighbouring plants. This is known as nitrogen fixing
* Covering the soil, minimising erosion, nutrient leaching and compaction
* Suppressing weeds
* Producing a mass of foliage that can be composted or dug in to improve soil structure and replenish soil nutrients
* Flowering early and/or lengthily through the growing season to bring beneficial insects to the garden

There's a big crossover between green manures and companion planting. In essence most green manures *are* companion plants, and this is particularly apparent in relation to fruit. They are a no-brainer for the organic grower – sow some green manures and while you enjoy the prospect of fruit, they set about quietly improving the soil structure, raising the nutrient status and attracting insects that pollinate your fruit plants and prey on potential pests.

You can use green manures across a whole field, in a small pot, or anywhere in between. Prepare the ground well, clearing it of all weeds and grass (see p.142). Sow evenly into a fine tilth before raking the seed in gently and shallowly. Water well.

The following table includes the green manures I think can work well with fruit, giving an idea of when to use them and the benefits they offer.

Green manure	Sow	Mow or dig in	Benefits
Alfalfa	May–July	Aug–Oct or overwinter	Nitrogen fixer. Very rich in main elements needed for good growth and draws up other trace elements from deep in the soil
Agricultural lupins	March–June	Sept–Nov	Flowers attract beneficial insects. Very deep-rooting, which helps to improve heavy soils and draw deep minerals to the surface. Nitrogen fixer; loves an acid soil
Buckwheat	April–Aug	July–Nov	Deep-rooting, attracts beneficial insects, good on poor ground (which it also improves)
Crimson clover	March–Aug	June–Nov or overwinter	Nitrogen fixer. If left to flower, will attract beneficial insects
Field beans	Sept–Nov	After winter	Nitrogen fixer. Excellent winter coverage for otherwise bare beds
Yellow trefoil	March–June	Sept–Nov	Nitrogen fixer. Low-growing with pretty small yellow flowers which bring bees to pollinate
Phacelia	March–Sept	June–Dec or overwinter in the South	Beautiful blue-purple flowers attract beneficial insects
Red clover	April–Aug	2 months after sowing or up to 2 years	Nitrogen fixer. Attracts beneficial insects
White clover	April–Aug	3 months or more after sowing	Nitrogen fixer. Low-growing plant. Attracts beneficial insects
Vetches	March–Oct	3 months after sowing but best overwintered	Nitrogen fixer. Likes a heavy soil

Controlling weeds

As with any plant you are cultivating domestically, you will need to keep on top of weeds. Nettles, docks and dandelions are a few of the plants that colonise ground quickly, often out-competing neighbouring plants to establish themselves in dense populations. You may find them unsightly but the primary downside of weeds is in robbing your fruit plants of precious resources – light, water and nutrients in particular.

Keep the competition to a minimum and your plants will establish more quickly; not only will they fruit sooner, they'll be better able to take care of themselves. With larger plants like trees and large shrubs, there will come a time when their size overcomes any competition weeds might offer, but in the early years of their life – and on an ongoing basis with smaller plants – weed control is really essential.

We have become lazy users of weedkiller, using a squirt or two of chemicals to kill off the nuisance weeds. Effective as this can be, weedkiller can also harm other plants and animals, unwittingly upsetting what is likely to be a perfectly happy, natural soil ecology in the process. There are a few organic, low-input methods of keeping the weeds at bay. And whether you spray or mulch (see p.175) or do neither, you'll find yourself having to manually remove any weeds that appear once in a while.

Manual weeding

With vegetables, a hoe is indispensable for slicing through the weeds that appear on the soil's surface, but many fruit plants, such as blackcurrants, have shallow roots that spread laterally from the plant and hoeing can cause damage. It's fine for very small weeds if the hoe's cutting action is kept shallow, but whereas vegetables are often grown in beds with relatively large, accessible lanes of bare soil separating the plants, fruit is often part of a more integrated garden and a hoe tends to be impractical.

The best way of tackling weed removal is to use a trowel – a narrow one is normally best, with sharp clean edges. You'll need to be diligent in digging down to the lowest of the roots if you want to be sure of getting rid of the weeds. This form of spot weeding may take a little time but it is very effective as you can be sure of removing all traces of the roots, which for perennial weeds such as docks is the only way of ensuring that they don't reappear. Do this as early as you can, when the plants are still young and small, and your work will be much, much quicker and easier. Whatever you do, don't let your weeds go to seed, get them early – if the wind gets hold of the seeds and spreads them through your garden, your battle will have multiplied enormously.

Strawberries grown through mulch mat

An even simpler method of controlling weeds is to smother them out before they have a chance to appear – using a mulch.

Mulching

A mulch is a layer of material on the surface of the soil that helps you and your crops by performing one or more of the following:

- Suppressing weeds
- Adding nutrients
- Retaining water in summer
- Reducing run-off in winter
- Improving soil structure
- Reducing temperature fluctuations
- Encouraging beneficial soil organisms
- Protecting edible crops that might otherwise touch the soil and rot (such as melons)

Mulches are pretty essential with most fruit plants, as weed competition – even for trees – can severely impede their development. With trees or large shrubs, or when planting in lines (such as a hedgerow), mulch mat provides an excellent long-term weed suppressant. You can buy it in 1m squares, as well as rolls of varying width and length.

Planting through mulch mat is simply a matter of making a small slit (if there isn't one in the mat already), planting through it, and turning the edges of the mat into the soil with the blade of a spade. Not only will the mat prevent weeds from draining the plant by competing with its roots, it will also help to retain moisture and keep the soil temperature up. Make sure you source mulch mat that is breathable and allows water through.

You can use manure or compost as a nourishing, as well as an effective mulch. Spread a 5–15cm deep layer of material around your plants to reap the benefits, having first watered the ground well to ensure that moisture is retained. Winter is an excellent time for applying a compost or manure mulch, as it allows nutrients to be incorporated into the soil before the new growing season.

If you can lay your hands on hay, straw, seaweed or spent mushroom compost, these are particularly good mulches. For larger expanses of otherwise bare soil, green manures (see p.171) or some of the companion herbs (see p.170) are your best options.

The same suppressing effect can be provided by gravel, tree bark, rubber chips and other bitty mulches. Choose whichever suits your garden, your sense of aesthetics and your pocket.

Pests and diseases

The best way of dealing with pests and diseases is through prevention. Maintaining a healthy soil, keeping up with pruning, growing green manures, companion planting and encouraging a diverse garden will all minimise the likelihood of pests and diseases, but once in a while they will appear. Knowing how to recognise and (if necessary) deal with them is vital, not only to the chances of getting a crop but potentially to the ongoing health of your plant.

The most common pests and diseases are covered in this section. If your chosen fruit is likely to be troubled by any of those listed, I have indicated the possibility in the Fruit A–Z (pp.28–121). A few problems that may affect only one or two fruit species are included in the relevant A–Z entries.

If you are troubled by larger creatures or birds, the main defence is obstruction. Rabbits and deer have to be fenced out of gardens, or for field-grown trees guarded against. Squirrels have to be trapped and dispatched, birds should be netted against, and/or scarers (such as CDs tied with string to flash in the sunlight) employed.

Aphids

Aphids affect many fruit, especially in early summer. In themselves they usually cause little damage, but they can harbour and transmit viruses, which may well impact more severely. Squash them when you see them and encourage predators such as ladybirds by planting a diverse garden.

Bacterial canker

Bacterial canker affects the *Prunus* family – cherries, almonds, peaches, plums, nectarines and apricots – and apples, revealing itself as small brown spots that turn into holes on the leaves. The following year the leaves may appear deformed, if at all, quickly discolouring and withering. Branches may begin to die back. This disease can potentially kill the tree. Cut back any affected areas and incinerate them as soon as you spot any trouble, and use a copper-based fungicide such as Bordeaux mixture in late summer, repeating at the start of autumn.

Birds

Birds are a somewhat random nuisance, wiping out a crop one year and totally ignoring it the next. Currants, cherries and berries are most susceptible. You can take the gamble, or you can net vulnerable plants as ripeness approaches.

Blossom wilt

Stone fruit, apples and pears are vulnerable to this disease, which shows itself by causing withered and rotting blossom. It can then continue into the plant through

Blossom wilt

Leaf curl (see p.178)

the foliage, causing considerable damage and weakening the plant, thereby making it susceptible to other attacks. Bordeaux mixture, sprayed just prior to flowering, is your best remedy. Cut out any affected areas and incinerate them immediately.

Botrytis

Botrytis is a grey, felty mould that can affect any part of the plant. It is most common in greenhouses and polytunnels when ventilation is poor and conditions are old and damp. It can also affect grapes as they approach ripeness. Maintaining good ventilation is the best preventative measure. Pick off any affected parts, as few effective fungicides are licensed for home use.

Brown rot

This fungal infection creates brown areas of rot in many kinds of fruit – apples, pears and many of the stone fruit in particular. The disease usually enters the plant through pest damage, so keep a good eye on your plants and ensure you prune with clean cuts. Remove and incinerate affected fruit immediately.

Brown scale

Sap-sucking insect, 2–4mm across, which causes leaves to turn yellow and die. Treat with an organic spray.

Codling moth

The larvae of this moth tunnels to the fruit's core to feed, not only spoiling some fruit but drilling a pilot hole for other pests such as wasps to take advantage of. Pheromone traps are available which attract and trap the males in late spring, leaving the females unmated.

Coral spot

This can affect many of the woody fruit, including figs, although the currants are particularly susceptible. Wet conditions encourage the disease; untidy pruning cuts do too. Orangy-pink spots appear on dead wood, which if not pruned out immediately, can spread down the plant. Act quickly, cutting out any affected areas and incinerating them.

Downy mildew

This appears as grey downy growth on the underside of leaves and yellow patches on the upper surface. It affects grapes and melons in particular. Ventilation, as with all mildews, is the key to reducing the likelihood of infection. Remove infected leaves and incinerate immediately. A sulphur-based spray (for suppliers, see Directory, pp.248–9) will help minimise damage.

Fireblight

A bacterial disease that blackens the leaves, shoots and flowers of apples, pears and quince. Affected areas look as if they've been burnt, hence the name. The bad news is it's incurable. So, you will need to prune off any affected area plus an extra 50cm or so of healthy growth and incinerate immediately. Disinfect secateurs after pruning each affected tree.

Fungal leaf spot

This can affect many fruit – berries and currants in particular – but it is very easy to identify, appearing on the leaves as purple-brown spots ringed with yellow. It can spread very quickly, weakening the plant considerably. Good ventilation, keeping humidity low, and removing and incinerating any affected leaves immediately is your best course of action.

Leaf curl

A fungal disease that affects peaches and nectarines, and almond trees, severely distorting the leaves (illustrated on p.177). Most trees drop affected leaves, leading to a loss of vigour and lack of fruit. Spring rains can encourage the disease; protecting trees during early spring can help, otherwise Bordeaux mixture may offer some remedy.

Mealy bugs

These small white insects, about 5mm across, may appear near the leaf axils and leaf midribs of grapes, figs and some citrus fruit. A sticky residue may be visible on the leaves, which often develop dark moulds. Biological controls are available for small or under-cover infestations. For outside remedies, use organic sprays.

Nectria canker

This tedious disease affects apples, making the bark crack and peel, causing sap leakage and dieback; it even kills off some trees. Prune out any affected areas, disinfecting your secateurs after dealing with each tree, and burning any diseased material. Bordeaux mixture sprayed in autumn offers a good degree of protection, and a quick spraying any time that you notice the infection may help arrest it.

Phytophtera

This is a fungus which can affect any woody fruit plant grown in a waterlogged area. It is easy to identify. After the plant has declined and died, the roots will often be orange in colour and smell sour. Don't replant in an area that has been affected and if you have only one alternative site with similar conditions, do improve the drainage before planting. There is no cure.

Powdery mildew

A fungal disease that affects leaves, which will look as if they are covered in a white powder. Affected leaves may turn yellow and deform. Good air circulation is vital in avoiding this disease. Powdery mildew can be a sign that the soil is too dry, so keep susceptible plants (like grapevines) from drying out. Remove any affected leaves and incinerate immediately.

Red spider mite

Infestations usually occur under cover where humidity levels are low, but they can also occur in dry conditions, such as where fruit is grown against a wall. You may notice dusty webs on the underside of leaves, along with yellowing and/or withering of leaves. Spraying the leaves and/or the floor of a polytunnel or greenhouse may help by raising the humidity levels. Biological controls and organic insecticides can remedy an infestation.

Rust

Plums and their close relations, pears and some of the berries are susceptible to rusts. Bright-orange blisters appear on the underside of leaves in summer, turning gradually brown. Plants can weaken considerably, so remove and incinerate any affected leaves.

Scab

Scab is apparent as brown or green spots on the leaves and shoots, and can lead to misshapen fruit. Some varieties offer a degree of resistance but if it appears then chemical sprays are your only redress.

Shothole

Stone fruit are vulnerable to this disease. As the name suggests, it appears as a peppering of small circular dots on the leaves, which turn to holes over summer. Shothole can indicate the presence of mildews and bacterial canker, so prune off badly affected leaves immediately.

Silver leaf

Silver leaf affects the *Prunus* family (apricots, cherries, peaches, nectarines, plums and damsons), giving leaves a silver sheen before they wither and die. Purply-brown fungal brackets can appear on the branches. Pruning in the summer when the sap is rising minimises the risk of your tree succumbing to silver leaf. If, however, it becomes affected, cut back the stem (you'll notice a brown stain running through the branch) to at least 15cm beyond any staining. There is no cure, but if you act early you may get lucky.

Slugs and snails

Slugs and snails are much less of a nuisance with fruit than they are with vegetables, but they can cause major problems for strawberries, melons and mulberries. Picking the creatures off at dusk is a good measure. You can also buy organic pellets, which curb their appetites rather than poison them, and slug pubs are particularly effective.

To make a slug pub, cut off the bottom 10–12cm of a plastic drinks bottle and sink it almost completely to soil level. Leaving 2cm or so above the soil ensures that beetles and other small animals don't fall in. Fill it with that awful 2 per cent beer. It attracts the molluscs, which fall in and expire. Tip them with the liquid onto the compost heap and refill. If you place a ridge roof tile over the slug pub it will keep the area dark and damp yet accessible – just how slugs and snails like it.

Viruses

There are any number of viruses that can affect fruit, most appearing as marbling, blotches or yellowing leaves. They can debilitate or even finish off your plant and for the most part they are incurable.

Source certified virus-free plants where possible, and keep greenfly under control as they can be effective carriers of many viruses. Incinerate any affected plants immediately.

Wasps

Wasps can be a complete nuisance. They love the easy pickings of raspberries and strawberries but will happily bore into apples, plums and pears amongst others, potentially causing huge damage to crops. Once they start on your fruit, their presence can make it tricky to harvest what's left. Wasp traps work well.

To make a wasp trap, dissolve a spoonful or two of jam in twice the amount of water, pour it into a jam jar and puncture a hole in the lid, large enough to allow wasps in but not too much larger. Empty every few days and keep redoing.

Winter moths

Caterpillars love to eat and can strip a plant of succulent leaves rapidly. Winter moth caterpillars can damage the leaves, buds and flowers of pears, cherries and plums in particular. If there's only the odd one, just keep an eye on things – birds will usually even things up naturally. If numbers increase or there are plenty of eggs, squish them sharpish. You can take preventative measures against some caterpillars by ringing the trunk with sticky strips from a horticultural supplier or even using a ring of Vaseline – the caterpillar can't work its way across either.

Woolly vine scale

Grapes and currants are most susceptible to this small flat brown insect, only about 5mm across. White woolly eggs covered in cottony threads laid in spring develop into the insect which feeds on the sap. Organic sprays are available.

Eyed hawk moth caterpillar

Growing in Containers
& Under Cover

Growing in containers or in a protected space, such as a greenhouse, can provide you with the opportunity of growing fruit where space or climatic limitations might not otherwise allow it. Some fruit take to container and under-cover growing better than others, but if you select the most suitable varieties and exercise a little care, both methods – growing fruit in containers and growing under cover – can produce great results.

Container growing

More and more people are growing fruit in pots, trugs, barrels and any other kind of container they can lay their hands on. And, happily, plant breeders are coming up with more varieties (including trees on dwarfing rootstocks) that are suitable for container growing.

While fruit tends to take very well to container growing, you may find that your plant does not produce the same yields as those grown in the ground. But if you haven't got the space, or you just prefer to keep your fruit in containers, you can still get a good, healthy harvest with a little care.

Container growing is also an excellent way (sometimes the only way) to overcome any limitations your soil may have. It also gives you the possibility of taking your plants indoors through the winter and even through early spring when some plants' flowers might be susceptible to frost damage.

There are some golden rules if you want to make container growing work for you. You'll need to start your plants off in ideal conditions, and then, equally importantly, keep up the love and attention.

Choosing containers

Trugs, wooden barrels, hanging baskets, old wellies, olive oil tins, raised beds and pots of terracotta, plastic, metal or wood: the list of containers in which you can grow fruit is as long as your imagination. Each has its own qualities, and you should really choose very much in line with your sense of what suits, what's around and any budget you may have. The only considerations you need to bear in mind are that your container should be large enough for the plant (see below), physically strong enough to cope with the combined weight of the plant(s) and moist compost, and have good drainage.

Put a plant into a sealed box and water will be unable to drain away. The compost will become waterlogged and the plant will decline and likely as not die rapidly. It's one of the critical balances of growing most plants. They will need a plentiful supply of water, but most prefer to sip regularly rather than drown in a bathful. Punch or drill holes into the base of your container if it has none.

Strawberries growing in a bucket

Don't try to squeeze a £20 plant into a 20p pot. Use a container that's large enough to accommodate your plant well. There should be some room for the roots to grow into, but don't make it too large. Over-potting does the plant no good at all. And keep it in mind that you'll need to move up a pot size at some stage. Allowing plants to outgrow their container and become pot-bound is the easiest and most common way of mistreating container plants. It slows them down, arrests development and productivity, and it can be tricky to get your plant to recover.

The rule of thumb is to plant your container fruit one or two pot sizes up from that which it was supplied in. If you've bought bare-root plants, make sure the roots have plenty of room – they shouldn't be cramped or squashed against the sides or base. Trees, bushes and energetic climbers need a pot with a minimum diameter of 38cm to start with, and may need potting on as the years pass into considerably larger containers, depending on type and rootstock.

Choosing compost

Start with good-quality potting compost. By 'good-quality' I mean peat-free, preferably organic, blended specifically for container growing, and sourced from a reputable supplier (see Directory, pp.248–9). This will give your plants the best growing environment they can have without contributing to the destruction of precious and declining peat habitats. You may want to add some grit for drainage. Some plants (such as blueberries) need a very specific growing medium; where this is the case, I've covered it in the Fruit A–Z (pp.28–121).

Planting in containers

Before you start piling in compost, put a layer of stones, gravel or broken pots into the bottom of your container to ensure water can drain away readily. Take your plant and just size it up in the pot. You'll want to plant it as deep in the compost as it was in the pot (or as deep as it was in the ground if it's a bare-root plant). You also want to leave 3–4cm between the top of the compost and the rim of the pot to allow for expansion when you water.

Scoop some compost into the container, but not too much – you are only trying to make a base for the plant to sit on to get it at the right height. Once that's accomplished, gently ease compost evenly around the plant, pushing it reasonably firmly in, to ensure no major air pockets, until the plant is happily snug.

Water well and, if you need to, add a little more compost if it has sunk around the sides of the plant. Once the water has been absorbed, you should still have that 3–4cm gap between the top of the compost and the rim of the container.

You can always add a layer of gravel, bark, or similar to the surface. This top dressing helps minimise weed growth, reduces evaporation and stops the surface of the compost solidifying in the sun.

Ongoing container care

A plant in a container is feeding off a limited well of resources. It should be perfectly happy, but only if you keep replenishing this well. Being awake to watering is essential. When your plant is in fruit you may need to water daily. You'll also need to be on top of feeding. Within a month or two most of the nutrients in your compost will have been exhausted, and you'll need to replace them. You have a few options when it comes to what you feed them with (see p.161) and, whatever you choose, fix a time to do it every week between April and the end of August. I say this because it's very easy to lose track of time and find your plants have been a few weeks without.

Apart from that, prune and care for your container plants as you would if they were growing in the soil.

Growing under cover

Our famously erratic climate can sometimes do with a little help to ripen the more marginal fruit. Grow your apricots in a greenhouse or polytunnel and your chances of fruit, and a hefty harvest thereof, are much increased. There is, however, a price to pay. You'll need to water more frequently, watch out for diseases, and as temperatures fluctuate over the year, you may need to move some plants into or out of your under-cover areas. But if you're prepared to do that you'll certainly open the door to a few otherwise uncertain harvests.

Advantages of growing under cover:
- Temperatures are raised under cover, meaning spring arrives earlier, winter comes later
- Summer temperatures are higher
- There is some degree of frost protection
- Some fruit that might otherwise be very unlikely becomes possible, and the marginal fruit more reliable
- Being grown under cover protects the plants that are susceptible to leaf curl from the spring rains that can encourage the disease
- Your structure not only protects the plants from the worst of the cold and rainy weather, it protects you – so you can carry on gardening
- Having a polytunnel or greenhouse allows you to grow container-grown plants outside during the summer and take them under cover for the colder months
- Watering using a sprinkler or drip-feed system is usually more practical to set up under cover

Drip irrigation

Things to bear in mind when growing under cover:

- Most plants will require more watering than if they were grown outside
- For most plants, good ventilation is vital to ensuring healthy development and keeping diseases to a minimum
- Summer temperatures can be too high for some plants

Preparation

Whether you are growing in containers or into the soil, preparation will be similar for growing under cover as outside. Take the same care over what you fill your container with (see p.186) and dig over and add organic matter to the soil as you would if you were planting out in the open. Think about how you plan on watering before you plant anything.

Watering and feeding under cover

If you think you're happy to water and feed your plants using watering cans, bear in mind you may need to do this at least once a day through the hottest part of the year. Overhead watering is an option but is much better suited to low-growing plants rather than leafy, tall trees, which will mostly deflect the spray away from the developing root zone. Seep hose has perforations along its length to gently release water at regular intervals and works reasonably well.

My preferred choice, however, is a drip system, where narrow pipes with small drop attachments junction off from the main water pipe and are held in place next to each plant by spikes. Keeping the water on a low pressure causes drops to pop out constantly from each narrow pipe and drip down the spike into the root zone. It's an efficient, low-cost system that takes the strain out of summer watering.

Do be mindful of different plants' watering requirements though. There are some (including most citrus) that prefer a drench once a week even if that leaves them dry between, whereas most other fruit prefer more consistent moisture.

However you water, but especially if you are using a watering can or overhead system, you'll need to increase feeding when growing fruit under cover. Extra watering takes the nutrients more rapidly out of the upper layers of the soil or potting compost. You'll need to liquid-feed every fortnight through the growing season and consider using a slow-release pelleted chicken feed or similar that will gently let its goodness out (see Directory, pp.248–9, for suppliers).

Hand pollination

Extending the growing season is one of the advantages of growing under cover. The protected conditions fool your plants into thinking spring has come a little earlier than it has outside. Growth starts early, as does flowering, and while being under cover gives the blossom protection, there are likely to be fewer pollinators

Aiding pollination with a soft brush

around as these flowers emerge. With limited pollination you are likely to get limited fruit – so you'll need to step in and help things along. A soft, small artist's brush is perfect for the job of gently brushing over the pollen-laden anthers of each blossom, gently transferring pollen from one flower to another as you go.

Dealing with too much heat

Greenhouses in particular can give you too much of a good thing – heat and light. While it helps your otherwise marginal fruit to mature more reliably, too much heat and harsh light can be stressful for your plants and provide ideal conditions for many pests. You can paint the glass of greenhouses with a shade paint, though this can be as tedious to remove as it is easy to apply. Shade netting works well although it is slightly fiddly to set up, but you'll still need to get doors and ventilation open early in the day. It's also well worth watering the floor – known as 'damping down' – as this increases humidity as the moisture evaporates in the heat, reducing the likelihood of numerous pests.

Polytunnels usually have a cloudier covering of semi-transparent plastic, which takes the edge off the heat without diminishing the light levels significantly.

Ongoing and winter care

With more heat and a longer growing season you are likely to have more plant growth, so you'll need to keep up with pruning to stop your plants becoming over-stretched and unproductive. You'll not need to do anything differently from what you'd do if the plants were growing outside, but you may have to get accustomed to taking more growth off when the time comes. With more vigorous growth, you may need to consider wires and/or canes, etc, to keep your plants supported.

When the heat has passed, you'll still have a few tasks to undertake. Most plants will lose their leaves through winter. Do keep on top of removing them, as they not only clutter the floor, they can also harbour disease that will affect your plants the following season. Add them to your compost heap or leaf-litter pile. Some plants (such as melons) that are annuals are grown just for one growing season and the whole spent plant will need removing once the fruit has been taken.

You may have to shuffle some plants around as the cold weather approaches. Move in any of your container-grown plants that would benefit from a warmer winter, protection through spring flowering, or keeping out of spring rains which can encourage leaf curl. You may also need to remove citrus plants if your greenhouse or polytunnel is unheated. These enjoy a minimum of 10°C, so you may have to bring them into the house or conservatory if you have one.

Towards the end of winter, top-dress containers with new compost along with slow-release natural fertiliser, and dig slow-release fertiliser and compost into the topsoil if you're growing fruit under cover in the ground.

Recipes

Orchard ice cream
with caramelised walnuts

Vary the combination of fruit according to taste and availability – my favourite is half apples, half quince – and try adding a little cinnamon before cooking. A touch of cream dribbled over the ice cream cuts the floral quince beautifully.

Serves 4–6

350g mixed apples, pears and/or
    quince (in any proportion), washed
60g unsalted butter
3 tbsp cider brandy (optional)
300ml double cream
1 vanilla pod, split lengthways
4 eggs yolks
140g caster sugar

For the caramelised walnuts
A couple of handfuls of shelled
    walnuts
2 tbsp honey
2 tbsp brown sugar
A good pinch of salt

Peel, core and chop the fruit. Put into a pan with the butter and 2 tbsp water. Cook gently, covered, until completely soft. Push the purée through a sieve if it appears too grainy (most likely if you've used a lot of quince). Add the brandy if using.

Pour the cream into a large saucepan, add the vanilla pod and bring to just below the boil, then take off the heat. Meanwhile, whisk the egg yolks and sugar in a bowl until creamy and thick. Remove the vanilla pod from the cream, then slowly pour onto the sugar/egg mixture, whisking as you do so. Return to the pan and cook gently, stirring constantly with a wooden spoon; don't let it boil. After 15–20 minutes the custard should have thickened enough to coat the back of the spoon.

Stir the custard into the fruit purée. Allow to cool completely, then chill. Churn in an ice-cream maker if you have one. (If not, freeze in a shallow lidded tub, beating with a fork every 45 minutes or so, for a smooth result.)

For the caramelised walnuts, preheat the oven to 180°C/Gas mark 4. Toast the nuts on a baking tray for 5–10 minutes; don't burn. Heat the honey and 2 tbsp water in a frying pan until bubbling, then add the walnuts, tossing to coat. Scatter over the sugar and salt. When the sugar has melted, toss the nuts again. Tip onto greaseproof paper, separating the nuts. Once cool, break apart any that are stuck together.

Before serving, soften the ice cream in the fridge for 30 minutes. Serve scattered with caramelised walnuts. Store the rest of them in a sealed tub for up to a week.

Lamb and apricot tagine

Don't be put off by the long list of ingredients: this is very simple to make. The many spices build up a lovely depth of flavour that brings out the best in the lamb and apricots. Avoiding browning the meat first is something I picked up from the wonderful Debora Robertson, who I worked with on *A Taste of the Unexpected*. Moroccans don't, and it makes for a straightforward, deliciously authentic dish.

As a variation, quince – quartered and poached for 30 minutes – work every bit as well as the apricots.

Serves 4–6

1kg shoulder of lamb, cut into 3cm chunks
1 cinnamon stick
2 tsp ground cumin
1 tsp sweet paprika
1 tsp hot paprika
1 tsp ground coriander
1 tsp ground turmeric
4 cardamom pods, lightly crushed
400g tin chopped tomatoes
2 onions, peeled and finely sliced
25g fresh ginger, peeled and grated
1 tsp saffron threads
1 tbsp tomato purée
2 tbsp olive oil

4 garlic cloves, peeled and finely chopped
500g fresh apricots, halved and stoned (or this quantity of dried apricots)
A little pared zest and the juice of 1 lemon
2–4 tbsp honey
Sea salt and freshly ground black pepper
A handful of coriander leaves, finely chopped, plus a few sprigs to garnish
A small handful of mint leaves, finely chopped
Lemon wedges, to serve

Put the lamb into a bowl, add all the dry spices and mix together well. Cover and leave to stand in a cool place for at least 3 hours.

Put the spiced lamb, tomatoes and onions into a large pot and add enough water to just cover. Bring to a simmer, then add the ginger, saffron, tomato purée, olive oil and garlic. Stir well, return to a simmer, then lower the heat. Cook very gently, with the lid partially on, for 2 hours.

Add the apricots, lemon zest and juice, and 2 tbsp honey. Cook gently for another 30 minutes, adding a little water if you think it is needed. Taste and season, adding a little more honey if you fancy. Stir in the chopped coriander and mint.

Serve garnished with coriander sprigs, with lemon wedges on the side. Accompany with Moroccan breads or rice.

Apricots on toast

This gorgeous, spicy and sweet snack works equally well with nectarines or peaches in place of the apricots. If you want to make a bit more of it, leave out the toast and serve the fruit as a dessert with a simple, not-too-sweet fresh raspberry sauce (see variation).

Serves 4

4 slices of white bread, crusts removed, cut into triangles
100g unsalted butter
120g runny honey

1 vanilla pod, split lengthways
4–6 cardamom pods
16 firm apricots

Preheat the grill to high and toast each slice of bread on one side.

Melt the butter and honey together in a small saucepan. Scrape out the vanilla seeds from the pod and add them, along with the pod and the cardamom pods, to the honey and butter. Increase the heat, bring to the boil and boil for 30 seconds. Remove from the heat.

Halve the apricots and remove the stones. Place them, skin side up, on a baking sheet and grill for a minute or two until they start to colour. Remove the baking sheet from the grill.

Lay the half-done toast, uncooked side up, on another baking sheet. Use a spatula to turn the apricots, cut side up, over onto the toast, spoon the honey butter over and grill for 3–5 minutes until soft and cooked through. Serve straight away.

Variation

Rather than have the apricots on toast, serve them with a raspberry sauce: pulse 200g raspberries with 2 tbsp caster sugar and 2 tbsp water in a food processor and sieve before pouring over the apricots.

Blackberry apple compote

I can't seem to make enough of this really delicious, slightly addictive compote. Once a jar has been opened in our house, it tends to appear on the table every breakfast time until it's gone. The mix can become very thick if you overcook it – something I do frequently – but I'm starting to prefer it that way. Even when thick, it doesn't seem like a jam, as the low sugar content ensures it doesn't become cloying, though that means it won't keep as long as most jams.

Makes 4 x 220ml jars

250g caster sugar
6 finely pared strips of lemon zest
2 cinnamon sticks
2 star anise

500g cooking or dessert apples,
    peeled, cored and sliced
250g blackberries

Put the sugar into a large pan with 550ml water and stir over a moderate heat until the sugar has dissolved. Add the lemon zest, cinnamon and star anise, then turn up the heat and bring the liquid to the boil. Reduce to a simmer.

Add the apples to the pan and cook gently for 5 minutes. Now add the blackberries and simmer until you have a smooth, thick compote. Spoon into several sterilised jars, fishing out the star anise, cinnamon and lemon zest as you go.

Seal the jars and store in a cool, dry place. The compote will keep for a few months but will need to be refrigerated once opened. Serve with yoghurt, with pancakes or drop scones, or in any other way you fancy.

Variations

Most fruit will make a fine compote but the berries, blackcurrants, pears, plums and apricots are perhaps the best. Apple and quince compote is particularly good: use 600g apple and 150g quince.

Frozen summer berries
and hot white chocolate sauce

This wonderful, simple pudding, made famous by the Ivy restaurant in London, exploits the contrast between hot and cold, sweet and sharp. Use any mix of your favourite berries and fresh summer currants. Personally, I would avoid using solely sharp currants – but if you like them, why not?

To keep berries and currants from freezing together into a solid lump, freeze them first spread out on a tray, then tip them into a bag once frozen.

Serves 4

200g good white chocolate, broken
    into small pieces
200ml double cream

1 tsp white rum (optional)
500g mixed frozen berries (and
    currants if you like)

For the sauce, put the chocolate and cream into a heatproof bowl over a pan of very gently simmering water, making sure the bowl isn't actually touching the water. Heat *very* gently for 10–15 minutes, stirring occasionally as the chocolate melts; the mixture will thicken steadily. Stir in the rum, if using.

A few minutes before serving, distribute the frozen berries among individual dishes – a few minutes at room temperature takes the edge off their chill.

When you're ready to serve, pour the hot white chocolate sauce into a jug and let everyone help themselves.

Summer pudding

When I first heard about summer pudding many years ago I couldn't have been less excited about the prospect. White bread, fruit, sugar, and the pudding wasn't even cooked: how good could that be? As good as any other pudding, I was soon to discover. Use whichever mix of currants and berries takes your fancy; just keep the total weight of fruit the same. The key to making the very loveliest summer pudding is to heat the fruit only until the sugar dissolves and the juices start to run, no longer.

Serves 4–6

500g raspberries
250g redcurrants
150g blackcurrants or blackberries

200g caster sugar
10 thick slices of good white bread,
    crusts removed

Put all the fruit and the sugar into a large saucepan and cook over a gentle heat for 4 minutes or so – just until the juices begin to run and the sugar is dissolved. Remove from the heat.

Line an 850ml pudding basin with a double layer of cling film, leaving plenty overhanging the rim. Line the bottom and sides of the bowl with bread slices, overlapping them slightly to ensure there are no gaps and keeping one slice back for the lid.

Drain 100ml of the juice from the fruit into a small bowl, cover and refrigerate. Spoon the rest of the fruit and its juice into the pudding basin. Place a slice of bread on top and fold over the cling film to seal the pudding. Place a saucer or small plate, which just fits inside the bowl, on top of the pudding and add a weight such as a bag or two of sugar, or some tins of food. Refrigerate overnight.

When you are ready to serve the pudding, lift off the plate and peel back the cling film. Place a serving plate over the top of the pudding and invert the pudding and plate carefully. Lift off the bowl and remove the cling film. Spoon the extra chilled juices over the pudding and serve with thick double cream.

Crème de cassis

Blackcurrants are one of those fruits that seem to take us by surprise. We want them for the many months they aren't in season, then run out of ideas for what to do with them when harvest time arrives. This is an excellent way to preserve their inimitable flavour to enjoy whenever you like.

A little homemade crème de cassis (about 1cm) in a wine glass topped off with white wine gives you the perfect kir and it's fantastic dribbled over ice cream or whirled through a cake mix. The leaves add a greater depth of flavour than the currants alone and contribute a delicious, gently spicy edge.

Makes about 2 litres

1kg blackcurrants
20 blackcurrant leaves

1 litre gin
650g granulated sugar

Wash the blackcurrants and pinch off their stalks. Dry the fruit thoroughly and put it into a large glass jar with the blackcurrant leaves. Pour in the gin and leave for at least 4 months.

Strain the gin into a large jug, discard the leaves and purée the blackcurrants in a food processor. Strain the blackcurrant pulp through a muslin-lined sieve and mix with the gin.

In a saucepan over a gentle heat, dissolve the sugar in 140ml water. Increase the heat and simmer gently for 5 minutes until the sugar syrup thickens. Remove from the heat and allow to cool completely.

How much of the sugar syrup you add to the fruity alcohol to sweeten it is up to you – add it in instalments, stirring and tasting regularly. Once it is as you like it, pour into sterilised bottles and seal. Although the liqueur will be delicious immediately, it will improve with age and it keeps indefinitely.

Blueberry muffins

This is a wonderful muffin recipe that also works deliciously with anything from alpine strawberries to currants. You can even throw in a few crushed nuts. The more adventurous should try adding half a teaspoonful of freshly ground coriander seeds when you add the blueberries – I know it sounds peculiar, but it works...

A few of these muffins, crumbled up, are perfect as the sponge element in a trifle (see p.244).

Makes 12

250g plain flour
2 tsp baking powder
½ tsp bicarbonate of soda
A good pinch of salt
120g unsalted butter, melted

120g caster sugar
2 eggs, lightly beaten
100ml full-fat milk
Finely grated zest and juice of 1 lemon
180g blueberries

Preheat the oven to 190°C/Gas mark 5 and line a 12-hole muffin tray with paper muffin cases. Sift the flour, baking powder, bicarbonate of soda and salt together.

In a separate bowl, beat together the butter, sugar, eggs, milk, lemon zest and juice until evenly combined. Gently fold in the flour mixture using a spatula, then fold in the blueberries; don't overmix.

Spoon the mixture into the muffin cases and bake for 16 minutes. To check, insert a cocktail stick into the middle of a muffin; if it comes out clean, they are ready, if not, give them another couple of minutes.

Transfer to a wire rack to cool. The muffins are best eaten the same day – ideally still slightly warm from the oven. Any that aren't devoured can be stored in an airtight container once they are completely cool and eaten the next day.

Variations

Blackcurrants, blackberries and alpine strawberries are all excellent substitutes for the blueberries in these muffins.

Cherry clafoutis

Clafoutis has long been one of my favourite puddings, but I was persuaded by Debora Robertson to cut back every gram of flour I possibly could to get the perfect combination of lightness, creamy centre and crisp top. As ever, she was right. This clafoutis is delicious with or without alcohol. Many liqueurs work well, but almonds and cherries were made for each other, so do give amaretto a try. The dusting of cocoa gives just a hint of chocolate that suits the cherries too.

Serves 6

20g unsalted butter, diced, plus
    extra for greasing the dish
75g plain flour, plus extra for dusting
A pinch of salt
½ tsp vanilla extract or seeds from
    ½ vanilla pod
1 tbsp amaretto, crème de cassis
    (see p.204) or kirsch (optional)

350ml whole milk
2 large eggs
40g caster sugar
300g cherries
1 tbsp cocoa powder
1 tbsp icing sugar

Preheat the oven to 230°C/Gas mark 8. Butter a round baking dish, about 25cm in diameter, or a rectangular one, about 28 x 20cm. Dust lightly with flour.

Sift the flour and salt into a large bowl and add the vanilla extract (or seeds), the liqueur (if using) and half the milk. Whisk to a smooth batter. Add the eggs, one at a time, whisking quickly as you add them. Now whisk in the caster sugar and the rest of the milk until the batter is just smooth.

Spread the cherries out in the baking dish, pour in the batter and dot the cubes of butter over the top. Bake for 25 minutes or until the batter is plump and golden.

Let the pudding stand for 5 minutes or so, then dust the cocoa over the surface, followed by the icing sugar. Serve warm, with double cream.

Variations

Many other kinds of fruit can be used instead of cherries but mulberries, pears, blueberries and plums are my favourites.

Baked figs with honey
and cardamom

Figs are wonderful baked. A brief time in the oven brings out their succulence and sweetness and they don't need much to help them along. You can leave out any of the spices and herbs if you like.

Serves 4

16 large fresh figs
2–3 tsp ground cinnamon or
    2 cinnamon sticks
3 cardamom pods, lightly crushed
3 tbsp runny honey

3 tbsp Marsala, Madeira, port,
    or water
3 thyme sprigs (or use lemon thyme
    if you have it)

Preheat the oven to 190°C/Gas mark 5. Cut the figs vertically into quarters, leaving them attached at the base. Squeeze each fig at the base to open them out a little. Stand the figs in a fairly small baking dish lined with greaseproof paper to prevent them sticking; they should be quite closely packed.

Dust over the ground cinnamon or add the sticks (whole or broken up) and sprinkle on the cardamom. Drizzle over the honey and alcohol or water, making sure some goes into the cuts. Scrunch up the thyme sprigs and throw over the figs. Roast in the middle of the oven for 15–20 minutes, depending on the size of the figs.

Serve warm with vanilla ice cream, or cream.

Variation
Plums, with their stones removed, are superb in place of the figs.

Gooseberry fool
with elderflower

A classic marriage of spring-into-summer flavours, as simple to make as it is delicious. You might like to top it off with a little cooked crumble mix (see p.239). Alternatively, serve it with almond tuiles, gingersnaps or shortbread.

Serves 4

500g gooseberries
4 tbsp caster sugar
2 finely pared strips of lemon zest

12 medium heads of elderflower,
plus a few to decorate
300ml double cream

Put the gooseberries into a pan with the sugar, lemon zest and a few splashes of water and throw the elderflower heads on top. Heat gently until the gooseberries begin to break up, then simmer for 15 minutes or so, stirring occasionally. Push the pulpy mush through a sieve and leave to cool completely.

Whisk the cream until soft peaks form, then fold into the gooseberry purée – either leaving it as a ripple or combining evenly. Refrigerate for a couple of hours before serving.

Spoon the chilled fruit fool into serving glasses and top each with a sprig of elderflower to decorate.

Variations
The various berries and currants, as well as rhubarb, will happily take the place of gooseberries.

Gooseberry tart

This is a fantastic tart that can easily be adapted to most berries and currants, although you may want to leave off the demerara for sweeter fruit, and the elderflower cordial unless you're using strawberries, which it pairs with beautifully. It is equally good with green or purple gooseberries, although I think it looks best with purple ones. Early-season gooseberries may call for a little more sugar.

Serves 6–8

For the pastry
200g plain flour
50g icing sugar
A pinch of salt
100g cold, unsalted butter, cubed,
    plus an extra knob of butter, melted
2 egg yolks

For the filling
100ml crème fraîche
2 egg yolks
1 tsp balsamic vinegar
40–60g caster sugar (see above)
500g gooseberries, topped and tailed
A little elderflower cordial (optional)
A few tsp demerara sugar

For the pastry, put the flour, icing sugar and salt into a food processor and blitz briefly to combine, or sift together into a bowl. Add the cubed butter and pulse, or rub in with your fingertips until the mixture resembles breadcrumbs. Lightly beat 1 egg yolk and stir it into the pastry, adding a few teaspoons of iced water at a time until the dough forms a ball. Wrap in cling film and refrigerate for 20 minutes.

Preheat the oven to 180°C/Gas mark 4. Dust your work surface and rolling pin with flour and roll out the pastry to a thickness of around 3mm. Use to line a 26–28cm tart tin placed on a baking sheet. Gently press the pastry into the base and sides of the tin, leaving any excess overhanging the rim. Prick the pastry base a few times with a fork and bake for 10 minutes. Lightly beat the other egg yolk, brush over the pastry and bake for a further 10 minutes. Trim off any overhanging pastry.

For the filling, whisk the crème fraîche, egg yolks, balsamic vinegar and sugar together. Scatter the gooseberries evenly in the pastry case and drizzle on a few drops of elderflower cordial if you fancy. Pour in the custard and sprinkle the surface evenly with the demerara sugar. Bake for about 40 minutes until the custard is set. Let the tart rest for 5 minutes before serving. Double cream is all it needs.

Variations

Stoned cherries, the currants and berries, roasted rhubarb and halved or quartered plums can be used equally well in place of the gooseberries.

Gooseberry curd

This is a variation on Pam Corbin's fantastic curd recipe. I love making it with purple gooseberries. They produce a lovely bright pink-purple curd, but green/yellow varieties are just as delicious. The curd is also good with apples in place of the gooseberries. For lemon curd, leave out the gooseberries, double the lemon juice and use the zest of 3 lemons.

Makes 5 x 225g jars

450g gooseberries, topped and tailed
Finely grated zest and strained juice
    of 2 unwaxed lemons (you need
    100ml strained juice)

125g unsalted butter, cut into cubes
450g granulated sugar
4–5 large eggs, well beaten (you need
    200ml beaten egg)

Put the gooseberries and lemon zest in a pan with 100ml water and cook gently until soft and fluffy. Leave to cool slightly, then rub through a nylon sieve, using a wooden spoon.

Put the sieved purée into a heatproof bowl with the lemon juice, butter and sugar. Stand the bowl over a pan of simmering water on a low heat. Heat gently, stirring, until the mixture is hot and glossy, then whisk in the eggs using a balloon whisk. Don't allow the mixture to overheat, otherwise it will 'split' and curdle when the beaten egg is added. If you have a sugar thermometer, use it to check the mixture goes no higher than 60°C. If the mixture does split, take the pan off the heat and whisk vigorously until smooth.

Once the eggs are incorporated, stir the curd over a gentle heat for 10 minutes or so until it is thick and creamy, using a spatula to scrape down the sides of the bowl every few minutes.

Pour the curd into warm, sterilised jars and seal. It will keep unopened for a month. Once opened, keep in the fridge and use it up fairly quickly.

Chicken Véronique

Chicken, wine, garlic, herbs and cream... retro perhaps, but the combination is so good. The late addition of the grapes adds an edge and texture to complement the wine flavour. This is one of those dishes that's very fine the following day too.

Serves 6

20g unsalted butter
4 tsp olive oil
1 free-range chicken, about 1.7kg
2 medium onions, peeled and finely sliced
3 garlic cloves, peeled and finely chopped
A bunch of thyme and/or tarragon

Sea salt and freshly ground black pepper
350ml white wine
2 or 3 bay leaves
250g white grapes, halved or whole
130ml double cream
A knob of soft unsalted butter, mixed with 1 tbsp plain flour (if needed)

Heat half the butter and half the olive oil in a large frying pan over a medium heat and add the whole chicken. Cook, turning from time to time, until you've browned as much of the bird as you can.

Meanwhile, heat the remaining olive oil and butter in a heavy-bottomed cooking pot (large enough to take the chicken) over a medium heat. Add the onions and sauté for about 10 minutes. Throw in the garlic and sauté for a couple of minutes.

Put the thyme and/or tarragon into the chicken cavity, then lay the bird on top of the onions and garlic and season well with salt and pepper. Pour in the wine and add the bay leaves. Bring up to a simmer, turn the heat down slightly, then put a lid on the pan and simmer gently for 1¾ hours.

Add the grapes and cook, uncovered, for another 10 minutes. Take the pot off the heat and, holding the chicken's legs with a cloth, lift the bird out onto a warm plate. Cover loosely with foil and leave to rest while you finish the sauce.

Return the pot to the heat and stir in the cream. If the sauce seems too thin for your liking, you can thicken it with the paste of softened butter and flour (known as beurre manié). Add it in little nuggets to the sauce, whisking or stirring all the time and allowing a minute or two for each addition to thicken the sauce. You may not need all of it. Once you've achieved the consistency you like, simmer gently for a further 2 minutes to cook the flour through. Taste to check the seasoning.

Carve or portion the chicken and serve with the sauce, potatoes and some greens.

Cranachan
with Japanese wineberries

Cranachan is a fantastic Scottish pudding, somewhere between a trifle and a fool, usually with raspberries at its heart. However, any berry or currant works well and Japanese wineberries, in my view, make the best cranachan of all. This is a pud to experiment with: adjust the sugar as you like, and try other spirits, liqueurs or sherry in place of whisky. My favourite version uses an Islay whisky such as Laphroaig – the smokiness sets off the toasted oats beautifully. Pungent heather honey is traditional but not essential – try other honey varieties.

Serves 4

50g rolled or porridge oats
2–3 tbsp whisky
3 tbsp caster sugar

300ml double cream
2 tbsp runny honey
350g Japanese wineberries

Gently toast the oats in a dry frying pan over a medium heat until golden; keep an eye on them as they can burn easily. Tip the oats onto a plate and leave to cool.

Stir the whisky and sugar together in a bowl, add the cream and whisk to soft peaks. Gently fold in the oats, honey and wineberries, aiming for a rippled effect rather than a complete blend. Don't worry if the berries bruise and leak a little of their juice: this adds to the beauty of the cranachan. Spoon into glasses and serve immediately.

Variations

Any of the berries, apples, plums and rhubarb can stand in for the Japanese wineberries, with gooseberries, apples, plums and rhubarb best poached to soften and even puréed first.

Medlar jelly

Medlar jelly is a fine accompaniment to rich meats. This deep amber preserve has just the right mix of sharp and sweet, with a fruity edge that I love. Unbletted medlars (see p.80) have a higher pectin content, while bletted ones have a deeper flavour – a mix of both is ideal. Don't throw away the leftover pulp – it adds a lovely datey flavour to chutneys (remove the seeds before using), and can be frozen.

Makes 4 x 225g jars

1kg medlars – ideally around half
   bletted, half not
½–1 lemon

About 500g granulated sugar
1 vanilla pod, split lengthways
   (optional)

Cut the medlars in half, or into quarters if large. Put them in a large pan and pour in just enough water to cover. Add the lemon juice (use the whole lemon for a sharper flavour). Bring to the boil, lower the heat and simmer for 1 hour. Give it an occasional stir but don't squash the medlars as this will make your jelly cloudy.

Now you need to strain the soft fruit through a jelly bag into a bowl; I do this overnight. If you haven't got a jelly bag you can use an upturned chair on a table (with the seat resting on the tabletop and the legs in the air). Tie the corners of a large square of muslin to the legs of the chair so the muslin forms a bag and allow the pulp to strain through into a bowl placed underneath. Don't squeeze or press the pulp down as your jelly will go cloudy.

Chill a small plate in the fridge. Measure the juice and pour it into a clean pan. For every 500ml, add 375g sugar. Add the vanilla pod, if using. Warm gently, stirring, until the sugar is dissolved, then increase the heat and boil, without stirring, for 5 minutes. Turn off the heat and test for setting: spoon a few drops onto the cold plate, leave for a minute, then push with your finger. It should wrinkle; if not, give it another 5 minutes and test again. Be prepared to test a few times as the pectin varies considerably with the degree of bletting that has occurred.

Pour the jelly into warm, sterilised jars and seal. It will keep in a cool, dark place for at least a year. Once open, store the jar in the fridge – it should still last for several months.

Variations

Quince, redcurrants and white currants all make deliciously different variations on this jelly.

Melon salad
with goat's cheese, mint and red onion

A delightful, fresh salad that works equally (though differently) with melon or watermelon, this is very adaptable. Try Caerphilly rather than goat's cheese, for instance, basil instead of mint, spring onions instead of red onion or a sharp, mustardy dressing in place of the chilli oil. It goes with so many things – fish especially – and is perfect as a barbecue side dish.

Serves 4

800g melon (or watermelon)
300g hard goat's cheese, sliced
   or crumbled
10 mint leaves, torn or chopped

½ red onion, peeled and thinly
   sliced
Chilli oil (or olive oil and a little
   finely chopped chilli)

Remove the skin and seeds from the melon (or watermelon) and cut the flesh into thick chunks. Mix or organise the melon, cheese, mint and onion as you like on a large serving plate, then drizzle with a little chilli oil.

Variation
Pears, either poached or perfectly ripe, can replace the melon.

Fruity melons

For this easy dessert, the only essential ingredient is the melon. The other fruit is very much up to you, although soft and ripe is ideal. You are looking for around 300g extra fruit, depending on the size of your melons.

Serves 4

1 large melon (or 2 medium, or 4 small ones)
1 ripe peach or pear, peeled and cut into 1cm dice or half-slices
A handful of grapes, deseeded, or cherries, stoned
A handful of raspberries and/or halved strawberries
3 tbsp caster sugar
2 tbsp lime juice
3 tbsp cider brandy, rum, dessert wine or port

Cut the top off the melon(s) and remove the seeds. Using a melon baller or spoon, scoop out as much flesh as possible (in balls if you can, but chunks are fine) without getting close enough to the skin to bruise it.

Put the melon flesh into a large bowl with the other fruit and add the sugar, lime juice and alcohol. Toss together.

Spoon the mixture back into the melon(s), put the top(s) back on and refrigerate for a couple of hours before serving.

Variations

The melons can be filled with whatever combination of fruit you fancy.

Mulberry mess

A classic Eton mess – made with raspberries and/or strawberries – is divine, but throw mulberries into the mix instead and you have what I think is one of the most gorgeous of all puddings. It's also brilliant with a blackberry apple compote (p.200) in place of the berries.

Serves 4

500g mulberries
40g caster sugar
350ml double cream

For the meringue
2 medium egg whites
100g caster sugar

Preheat the oven to 120°C/Gas mark 1 and line a baking sheet with baking parchment.

To make the meringue, put the egg whites into a clean bowl and whisk until they form soft peaks. Add half the sugar and whisk until it is completely incorporated. Add the rest of the sugar gradually, whisking until the mixture is thick, glossy and forms stiff peaks.

Spoon the meringue into smallish mounds on the baking sheet, spacing them apart to allow room for expansion. Bake in the centre of the oven for 2 hours. The meringues should be crisp on the outside and lift off the paper easily. They should be squidgy in the centre but you'll have to wait until you eat them to find out for sure! Transfer the meringues to a wire rack and leave to cool completely.

While the meringues are in the oven, put the mulberries into a large bowl with the 40g sugar, cover and leave to macerate in the fridge.

Any time up to an hour before you want to serve the pudding, lightly whip the cream. Break the meringues into pieces and fold them into the cream. Now fold in the fruit but not too thoroughly – this should be a marbled 'mess' rather than a thorough blend. Spoon into glasses and you're ready to serve.

Variations

Any of the berries – or apples, plums or rhubarb – can replace the mulberries. Gooseberries, apples, plums and rhubarb are best softened or even puréed first.

Peach salsa

This lively salsa is wonderful with fish, chicken or lamb, especially at a barbecue. It's beautifully adaptable too: the key thing is to include fruitiness, acidity, spicy punch and something aromatic. How you achieve this mix is up to you. The recipe works equally well with nectarines instead of peaches, for instance. You could also leave out the tomatoes, replace the spring onions with finely sliced red onion, or tinker with the herbs.

Serves 4–6

2 peaches (or nectarines), halved and stoned
1 ripe tomato, halved and deseeded
2 spring onions, trimmed and finely sliced
Juice of 1 lime
½ tsp caster sugar

1 small chilli (such as habañero), seeds and membrane removed, finely sliced
A small bunch of coriander, larger stalks removed, roughly chopped
5 mint sprigs, chopped
Sea salt and freshly ground black pepper

Cut the peaches and tomato into 5–7mm cubes. Simply toss together with all the other ingredients in a large bowl and season with a pinch or two of salt and plenty of pepper. The salsa is at its best if left for 10 minutes before serving.

Variation
Firm plums are a fine substitute for the peaches.

Pear and rocket salad
with Blue Vinny and walnuts

Each of the main ingredients here forms a happy partnership with any one of the others, so bringing the four together makes for a wonderfully harmonious whole. If I wanted to change this at all, I might consider adding a little extra edge with more mustard or some chopped chilli in the dressing. I've also used poached quince instead of pears, watercress in place of rocket, and hazelnuts rather than walnuts. You're not limited in your choice of blue cheese either – any good, salty one will work.

Serves 4

A handful of shelled walnuts
A few good handfuls of rocket
  (about 150g)
3 ripe pears
180g Blue Vinny or other blue cheese,
  crumbled
A dozen or so mint leaves, finely
  sliced (optional)

For the dressing
Juice of 1 lemon
1 tsp English grain mustard
Sea salt and freshly ground
  black pepper
5 tbsp extra virgin olive oil

Toast the walnuts in a hot, dry frying pan until golden, shaking the pan regularly to ensure the nuts don't burn.

For the dressing, put the lemon juice, mustard and some seasoning into a small bowl. Whisk in the olive oil. Taste and add more seasoning if you like. Pour half of the dressing into a large serving bowl and add the rocket. Turn it through the dressing until a thin slick coats the leaves.

Peel the pears and, holding each one by its stem, slice thinly, discarding the middle slice with the core. Add to the rocket with the cheese and walnuts. Scatter the sliced mint, if using, over the lot. Drizzle with the remaining dressing and serve.

Variations
Cherries, perfectly ripe figs, peaches or nectarines, or poached quince can replace the pear.

Poached pears
and chocolate sauce

This gorgeous dessert makes the most of under-ripe pears or cooking varieties. The spices are yours to alter, and you can poach the pears in half wine or cider and half water. The cooking time will vary depending on the variety of pear and degree of ripeness. Conference are ideal because they won't fall to pieces as softer varieties can. The pears will keep in their poaching liquor for up to 5 days in the fridge.

Serves 4

250g caster sugar
8 firm pears, peeled
1 cinnamon stick
½ tsp cloves
½ vanilla pod, split lengthways
½ tsp black peppercorns (optional)
½ lemon (optional)
2 star anise (optional)

For the chocolate sauce
170g dark chocolate, broken into
   small pieces
80g unsalted butter, cubed

Dissolve the sugar in 700ml water in a large saucepan over a medium heat. Add the pears and all the flavourings. The fruit must be completely submerged; add a little more water if needed. A 'cartouche' (a circle of baking parchment with a small hole cut in the centre) laid on the surface of the liquid will keep the pears submerged. Adjust the heat so the liquid is at a gentle simmer and cook for 15 minutes.

Meanwhile, make the chocolate sauce. Melt the chocolate and butter in a heatproof bowl set over a saucepan of simmering water, stirring occasionally. Once smooth, remove from the heat but leave the bowl over the water to keep the sauce warm.

Test the pears with a sharp knife – they should feel tender. If necessary, simmer for a few minutes longer. Once cooked, take the pan off the heat and allow the pears to cool a little in the liquid. If you prefer a sweeter, more intense syrup, transfer the pears to a warm bowl and reduce the liquid by boiling for a few minutes.

Serve the pears while still warm, bathed in a few spoonfuls of the aromatic syrup and the chocolate sauce. Clotted cream and/or shortbread are perfect on the side.

Variations
Try using quince. A combination of pear and quince is particularly special.

Plum and hazelnut cake

I love cakes that include ground almonds as well as flour. They have a fantastic fudginess and almondy background that is especially good paired with any of the stone fruit.

Serves 8

150g unsalted butter, softened, plus extra for greasing
150g caster sugar
3 eggs, lightly beaten
65g plain flour
1 tsp baking powder

110g ground almonds
60g hazelnuts, lightly toasted and crushed
16 plums, stoned and halved (quartered if very large)

Preheat the oven to 180°C/Gas mark 4. Lightly grease a 20cm round cake tin and line the base with baking parchment.

Beat the butter and sugar together until light, pale and creamy. Gradually work in the beaten eggs, adding a spoonful of flour at the same time to guard against curdling. Sift the remaining flour with the baking powder over the mixture and fold in lightly, using a large metal spoon. Now fold in the ground almonds, followed by the crushed hazelnuts.

Spoon the mixture into the prepared tin. Arrange the plums over the surface (you may have a few spare depending on the size of your plums); they will sink in a little as the cake cooks. Bake in the middle of the oven for 40 minutes, then test with a skewer – if it comes out clean, the cake is ready. If not, return to the oven for an extra 5 minutes or so.

When the cake comes out of the oven, allow it to rest for 10 minutes before removing from the tin. It's good cold but fabulous still warm, with clotted cream.

Variations

You could substitute peaches, cherries, gooseberries or even chunks of pear or apple for the plums, and replace the hazelnuts with walnuts.

Quince vodka

This is a wonderful way to enjoy quince months after the aroma of the ripening fruit has left the house. The basic recipe makes a lovely drink but one or more of the optional aromatics will give it a bit of a twist.

Makes about 800ml
2 large ripe quince
125g caster sugar
3 cinnamon sticks, 20 cloves and/or
**   a few sprigs of fennel (optional)**
700ml vodka

Wipe the quince, removing any fluffy down from the skin. Grate the fruit into a large, sterilised jar, picking out any pips. Add the sugar along with any of the aromatics you fancy. Pour over the vodka. Seal the jar and invert it a few times to mix the ingredients.

Leave the vodka for 2 months, inverting the jar every now and then when you remember. Taste and add a little more sugar if you like.

Leave it for another 2 months before straining it through a sieve, ideally through a funnel and back into the original vodka bottle. If you are impatient, you can drink it straight away but if you leave it a few months longer, a year if you can, the flavour will only improve.

Variations
Blackcurrants, the berries (apart from gooseberries), pears and plums all work well in place of the quince.

Raspberry fruit leather

This unusual preserve works well with almost any fruit. Don't be put off by the long cooking time. The method is as simple as it gets and the result is an intensely flavoured snack – one of the best ways I know to enjoy the flavour of a fruit long after the harvest.

Use this recipe as a template for other fruit leathers. Essentially, you just need to make a thick, smooth, gloopy purée of your chosen fruit and sugar and then dry it out very slowly in the oven until you have a pliable leather as clear and vivid as a stained glass window. Remember to add lemon juice if you are using fruit that is likely to discolour.

Makes 2 sheets, roughly 20 x 30cm
500g raspberries
500g peeled, cored and chopped
    cooking apples

Juice of 1 lemon
About 150g runny honey

Preheat the oven to 70°C/Gas mark ¼. Line two baking sheets (about 24 x 30cm) with baking parchment.

Put the raspberries, apples and lemon juice into a large pan. Bring to a low simmer then partially cover the pan and cook gently for about 20 minutes until pulpy. Allow the mixture to cool a little then push it through a sieve with the back of a spoon or pass it through a mouli. Weigh the purée. You should have about 750g. Add one-fifth of the weight of purée in honey and mix well.

Divide the purée between the two baking sheets, gently tipping the sheets to spread the mixture to the edges if it helps. Dry in the oven for 8–10 hours or until slightly tacky but not sticky, and easy to peel from the paper.

Leave the leather to cool completely, then tear it into pieces and store in a plastic tub, or roll it up in greaseproof paper or cling film and store in an airtight container. Either way, keep in a cool place and use within 3 months. The leather can also be frozen in a sealed container, for up to a year.

Variations
Most of the fruit in this book lends itself to leather (see above). The berries, apricots, peaches and nectarines work particularly well.

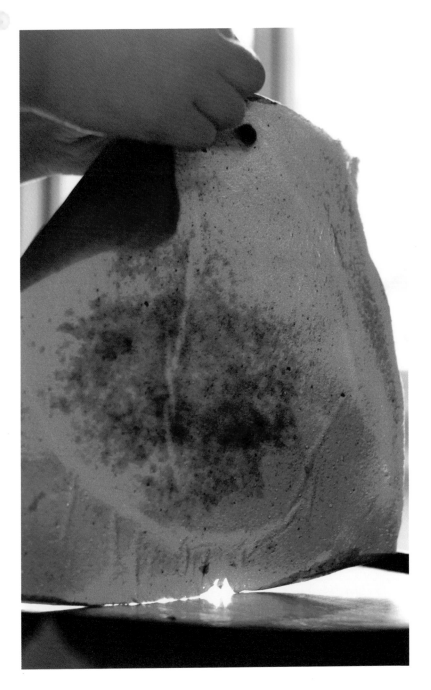

Bottled raspberries

Bottling is an old-fashioned way of preserving fruit – very simple, very good and much overlooked. It is essentially keeping fruit under liquid, such as a syrup made with sugar or honey. A little alcohol is a good addition too – brandy is lovely with raspberries. This is a variation on a recipe from Pam Corbin's *Preserves* handbook.

The following method works for most fruits, although you might want to use less sugar for sweet fruit, more for sharp or tightly packed fruit. You can also consider aromatics, such as cinnamon, cloves, sweet cicely and star anise. A few leaves of basil or mint add a lovely background note to these raspberries. And you can always combine fruits: half raspberries, half figs is a wonderful pairing.

Makes 6 x 225g jars
180g caster sugar
1kg raspberries (or 500g raspberries, 500g figs)

A few basil or mint leaves (optional)
150ml brandy (optional)

To make the syrup, put the sugar into a large pan with 700ml water and dissolve over a medium heat, stirring constantly.

Fill 6 sterilised screw-top or Kilner jars with the raspberries, handling the fruit carefully and making sure you don't compact it. Add the basil or mint and pour 25ml brandy into each jar, if using. Now pour in the hot syrup, filling the jars to the brim. If using screw-top jars, screw on the lids, then undo them half a turn – this allows steam to escape when they are in the pan. If you are using Kilner jars, rest the rubber seals and lids in place but don't fasten them down with the clips.

Stand the jars in a pan that is deeper than the jars and fill the pan with warm water, completely covering the jars. Bring the water up to simmering point very slowly, ideally over 30 minutes, and, once there, keep it simmering for 2 minutes. Remove from the heat. Once cooled a little, remove the jars and sit them on a folded tea towel to cool and dry completely. Tighten screw lids when they are cool enough to handle. The seal is critical, so if you're using Kilners, lift them carefully by the lid – if the whole jar lifts, the seal is tight and you can fasten the lids with the clips.

Store for up to a year in a cool, dark cupboard. Once opened, refrigerate and eat within a week.

Variations
Cherries, figs, plums, the berries and currants are all delicious bottled.

Rhubarb crumble

I love this almond crumble topping, with its shortbread-like fudginess. Putting the ginger into the topping rather than in with the rhubarb works a treat. If you're not familiar with sweet cicely, do give it a try; it's a herb that's very easy to grow. As well as adding a lovely aromatic edge to a dish, the aniseedy leaves make tart fruits seem sweeter, which means you can use less sugar.

Serves 4

750g rhubarb, trimmed
3 tbsp finely chopped sweet cicely
    leaves or 3 tbsp caster sugar

For the crumble topping
200g plain flour
A pinch of salt
140g caster sugar
2–4 tsp ground ginger, to taste
250g flaked almonds
200g cold, unsalted butter, cubed

Preheat the oven to 180°C/Gas mark 4. For the topping, put the flour, salt, sugar and ginger together into a food processor and blitz briefly to combine. Add the flaked almonds and process just enough to break them up but not turn them to dust. Add the butter and process until well mixed. The crumble should be in fudgy clods rather than in fine crumbs or, conversely, in one solid lump. Getting this right may take a little tweaking as the almonds can vary considerably. If the mix is too dry, add a little more butter; if it's in one or two lumps, add a little flour.

Cut the rhubarb into 5cm lengths, spread evenly in a baking dish and sprinkle with the sweet cicely or sugar. Scatter the clods of crumble mix fairly evenly over the fruit, letting them sit where they fall rather than pressing them down. Bake in the centre of the oven for 30 minutes or until the topping is golden with a few darker brown patches. Serve with cream or custard.

Variations

Apple crumble is the obvious variation on this recipe, and the pairing of apple with blackberries. But do also try apple in tandem with a few handfuls of raspberries or blueberries, or with a few slices of fragrant quince. Plums, mulberries, gooseberries and even apricots make lovely crumbles too.

Rhubarb and strawberry tart

The combination of strawberries, rhubarb and fresh ginger makes this one of the tastiest tarts I know, and the lack of a custard makes it one of the easiest.

Serves 6–8

For the pastry
200g plain flour
50g icing sugar
A pinch of salt
100g cold, unsalted butter, cubed,
    plus an extra knob, melted
2 egg yolks

For the filling
180g rhubarb, trimmed
200g strawberries, hulled and halved
40ml white wine
100g caster sugar
1 tbsp cornflour
1 tsp lemon juice
½ tsp grated fresh ginger

For the filling, cut the rhubarb into 3cm lengths and place in a large bowl with the strawberries, wine, sugar, cornflour, lemon juice and ginger. Toss to combine and leave to macerate while you make the pastry.

Put the flour, icing sugar and salt into a food processor and blitz briefly to combine, or sift together into a bowl. Add the cubed butter and pulse, or rub in with your fingertips, until the mixture resembles breadcrumbs. Lightly beat 1 egg yolk and stir into the pastry, adding a few teaspoons of iced water at a time until the dough forms a ball. Wrap the pastry in cling film and refrigerate for 20 minutes.

Preheat the oven to 180°C/Gas mark 4. Dust your work surface and rolling pin with flour and roll out the pastry to a thickness of around 3mm. Use to line a 26–28cm tart tin placed on a baking sheet. Gently press the pastry into the base and sides of the tin, leaving any excess overhanging the rim. Prick the base a few times with a fork and bake for 10 minutes. Lightly beat the other egg yolk, brush over the pastry and bake for a further 10 minutes. Trim off any overhanging pastry.

Using a slotted spoon, fill the tart with the fruit. Add 5–6 tbsp of the liquid too, but do not overfill. Stand the tin on a baking sheet and bake on a low oven shelf for 45 minutes–1 hour, until a golden crust forms and the liquid has set; it will thicken a little more as it cools. Let the tart cool before removing it from the tin. Serve with crème fraîche or double cream.

Variations
Any of the berries (apart from gooseberries) can replace the strawberries.

Strawberry granita

I've pinched the basics of this recipe from Hugh's *River Cottage Everyday* book. I love it mostly because it is so delicious but also because a granita is such a very simple and quick way to turn a glut of fruit into a fabulous frozen pudding without the need for an ice-cream maker. The texture is crunchy, the flavour sweet-tart and the experience deeply refreshing. You can try the recipe with any berries, stone fruit or even rhubarb, adjusting the sugar and lemon to suit.

Serves 8
1kg strawberries, hulled
200g icing sugar
Juice of 1–2 lemons

Put the strawberries in a large bowl and crush with your hands, then tip into a nylon sieve and rub them through to get rid of the seeds.

The amount of sugar and lemon juice you now add will vary depending on the variety of strawberries, their ripeness and your taste. I'd whisk in 140g sifted icing sugar and the juice of 1 lemon to start with, then taste and adjust. The key with most frozen puddings is to add more sugar and lemon juice than you think you need as both those tastes are muted on freezing. Pour the fruit purée into a plastic tub and freeze until solid.

Allow the granita to soften for approximately 20 minutes at room temperature, then take a strong fork to the surface, scratching and chipping it into a mass of shards and crystals. Pile your frosted scrapings into individual glass bowls and serve immediately.

Strawberry trifle

I couldn't write this book and not include a trifle recipe. This one brings together strawberries and elderflower, one of the loveliest fruity pairings. Any berries (except perhaps gooseberries), or currants, or even roasted rhubarb, can replace the strawberries. For a touch of luxury, finish with dark or white chocolate curls.

Serves 6

For the custard
4 egg yolks
1 heaped tbsp caster sugar
1 tbsp cornflour
350ml whole milk
1 vanilla pod, split lengthways

For the fruit
700g strawberries, halved if large
3 tbsp icing sugar

For the sponge base
4 muffins, plain or fruited (see p.207),
    or other cake, or sponge fingers
25ml strong elderflower cordial
125ml white wine or water

For the topping
440ml double cream, whipped, or half
    mascarpone/half double cream
A handful of toasted hazelnuts,
    roughly chopped

For the custard, mix the egg yolks, sugar and cornflour together in a bowl until smooth. Pour the milk into a heavy-based saucepan. Scrape the seeds from the vanilla pod with the tip of a knife into the milk and add the pod too. Bring to just below the boil. Take off the heat, discard the vanilla pod, then slowly pour the milk onto the egg mix, whisking constantly. Pour back into the pan. Cook gently, stirring constantly, for 5–10 minutes until thickened; do not allow to boil. Pour the custard into a bowl and cover the surface with cling film or greaseproof paper to prevent a skin forming. Leave to cool completely.

Put half the strawberries into a bowl, dust with the icing sugar and mash lightly.

Break the muffins or cake into big chunks and use to cover the base of a large glass bowl, placing the rest around the side. Dilute the elderflower cordial with the wine or water and drizzle over the sponge. Allow to stand for a few minutes.

Mix the lightly crushed strawberries with all but a dozen of the intact berries and tip them into the cup formed by the cake pieces. Spoon on the custard, levelling the surface. Whip the cream or whisk the mascarpone and cream together until smooth, then spoon on top of the custard. Dot with the remaining strawberries and scatter over the toasted hazelnuts. Refrigerate until ready to serve.

Useful Things

Directory

Plants and seeds

There are many good suppliers across the country. Those listed below are, for the most part, small to medium-sized businesses that I can recommend, having dealt with them personally.

Otter Farm Shop
www.otterfarmshop.co.uk
Modesty almost prevents me from telling you about this excellent range of fruit trees, bushes and seeds, including trained fruit and green manure seeds

Blackmoor Fruit Nursery
www.blackmoor.co.uk
01420 477978
Excellent range of fruit, including rootstocks

Reads Nursery
www.readsnursery.co.uk
01508 548 395
A wide range of fruit, including unusual varieties

Talaton Plants
www.talatonplants.co.uk
01404 841166
A wide range of fruit, with excellent varieties

Thornhayes Nursery
www.thornhayes-nursery.co.uk
01884 266746
Supplier of quality fruit trees, many uncommon varieties

Victoriana Nursery
www.victoriananursery.co.uk
01233 740529
Fine range of plants and seeds

Agroforestry Research Trust
www.agroforestry.co.uk
Diverse range of plants and seeds. Also courses

Other supplies

Fertile fibre
www.fertilefibre.com
01432 853111
Organically certified peat-free compost and more

Harrod Horticultural
www.harrodhorticultural.com
0845 402 5300
Wide range of fruit (and general garden) supplies, including excellent fruit cages

The Natural Gardener
www.thenaturalgardener.co.uk
01568 611729
Coir and biodegradable pots, compost and sustainable pest control

LBS Garden Warehouse
www.lbsgardenwarehouse.co.uk
01282 873370
General garden supplies, including mulch mat/ground cover and soil-testing kits

World of Felco
www.worldoffelco.co.uk
020 8829 8850
The best secateurs

Implementations
www.implementations.co.uk
0845 330 3148
Bronze/copper tools – hardwearing
and beautiful

Green Gardener
www.greengardener.co.uk
01493 750061
Extensive range of biological pest
control, plus general veg patch supplies

Rooster Pelleted Manure
www.rooster.uk.com
01325 339971
Pelleted manure (non-battery chickens)

Useful organisations

Garden Organic
www.gardenorganic.org.uk
024 7630 3517
Charity dedicated to organic growing.
Join to get access to a wealth of advice.
Also an excellent source for seeds and
everything to do with growing

Slow Food
www.slowfood.org.uk
020 7099 1132
Promoting the locality, diversity
and enjoyment of food

Royal Horticultural Society
www.rhs.org.uk
0845 062 1111
A great source of advice, with
numerous excellent gardens to visit;
also offers a soil analysis service

The National Fruit Collection
www.brogdalecollections.co.uk
01795 533225
Tours, events, courses and
identification of varieties

Reference books

You should find all the information
you need to grow your own fruit in
this handbook. If you're looking to
grow something a little more unusual
then allow me to immodestly steer you
towards *A Taste of the Unexpected*,
by myself.

If you're looking for more ideas for
what to do with your harvest, then
Pam Corbin's River Cottage *Preserves*
handbook is utterly indispensable.

For a wealth of wonderful fruit recipes,
plus much more, try Jane Grigson's
Fruit Book. And Niki Segnit's *The
Flavour Thesaurus* is a beautifully
written source of ideas for which
flavours might work well together.

Acknowledgements

Writing a book about fruit – with all the growing, eating and drinking involved – is a pretty pleasurable way of spending your time. While I do that, everyone else tries to make what I've done look great. If only life was always like that.

Here's where I say thank you.

I am hugely grateful for the way Richard Atkinson and Natalie Hunt at Bloomsbury have dedicated themselves to making this book as good as it possibly can be. To Janet Illsley, for her sensitive and insightful editing. To Toby Atkins, for his excellent illustrations. To Nikki Duffy, for her thoughts on the recipes. And to Will Webb, a designer whose wonderful eye just gets finer. This book has been a collaboration with you all, so thank you for your vision and enthusiasm.

Enormous thanks also to my agent, Caroline Michel at PFD, whose energy and ideas make such a difference.

To everyone at RCHQ, thank you for making going to work such a pleasure. Particular thanks to Ali Thomson, Kate Colwell and Michelle Wheeler, who make up the finest garden team anyone could wish for. Thanks to the kitchen team, especially Neil Matthews, Nonie Dwyer, Piers Harrison and Head Chef Gill Meller, who make it impossible to walk through the kitchen without picking up ideas as well as an extra inch or two to the waist. Steven Lamb: you great fool. To Rob Love, some fruit to go fishing with. And, of course, huge thanks to Hugh who somehow made River Cottage happen.

Coming up with recipes for fruit isn't too tricky – if you involve cream and/or meringue something marvellous generally follows. Going further and exploring fruity preserves and booze is equally rewarding and I am lucky to have Pam Corbin and John Wright as colleagues and friends. Thank you.

Lastly and most importantly, Candida and Nell – thank you for giving me the time and freedom to write this, as well as the reason to be growing it all in the first place. And to my mum, dad and sis for those distant memories of blackberrying before I could ride a bike.

Index

Page numbers in *italic* refer to the illustrations

River Cottage Handbooks

Seasonal, Local, Organic, Wild

FOR FURTHER INFORMATION AND
TO ORDER ONLINE, VISIT
RIVERCOTTAGE.NET